THE
Airbnb
MILLIONAIRE
MANIFESTO

UNVEILING THE MIND-BLOWING
WEALTH SECRETS OF AIRBNB

MIA CASHMAN

Table of Contents

Introduction:

Picture this: A world where your spare bedroom becomes a ticket to financial freedom, where meeting new people from all corners of the globe is just a part of your everyday life, and where your humble abode transforms into a sought-after destination. Welcome to the thrilling world of Airbnb, where the sharing economy meets extraordinary potential.

In recent years, the concept of sharing has taken on a whole new meaning. No longer confined to trading a cup of sugar with your neighbor, the sharing economy has exploded into a phenomenon that's shaking the foundations of traditional industries. And at the forefront of this revolution is Airbnb.

How Airbnb Has Transformed Travel and Hospitality

Gone are the days of bland, cookie-cutter hotels and uninspired accommodations. Airbnb has single-handedly breathed life into the travel and hospitality industry. It's a platform that's all about you - yes, you! Instead of simply booking a place to stay, Airbnb invites you to immerse yourself in the local culture, to live like a local, and to create unforgettable memories.

Imagine staying in a charming treehouse in the heart of a lush forest, a cozy cottage nestled in a picturesque village, or even a luxurious penthouse with panoramic city views. With Airbnb, your options are as diverse as the world itself. From quirky to opulent, from rural retreats to urban oases, Airbnb offers a universe of choices that traditional hotels can only dream of.

But Airbnb isn't just about providing unique places to stay; it's about connecting people. It's about forging bonds with hosts who are passionate about sharing their spaces and their stories. It's about opening doors to travelers who seek more than just a room; they crave experiences, authenticity, and a sense of belonging.

The Promise of Financial Freedom

Now, let's talk about the juicy part: financial freedom. Airbnb isn't just a platform for travelers; it's a goldmine for savvy individuals like you. You have the power to transform your property into a lucrative source of income. Whether you own a spare room, a vacation home, or an entire apartment building, Airbnb can turn your idle assets into a financial powerhouse.

This book is your ticket to unlocking the secrets of Airbnb wealth. It's a guide that will take you from newbie to Airbnb mogul, teaching you everything you need to know to thrive in this exciting landscape. Whether you're an empty-nester looking to fill your nest egg, a wanderlust-driven traveler, or a budding entrepreneur, the possibilities are endless.

Who This Book is For

Now, you might be wondering if this book is for you. Well, the short answer is yes! Whether you're a tech-savvy millennial, a retiree with a penchant for adventure, a family looking to boost their income, or an aspiring property mogul, there's a place for you in the Airbnb universe. This book is your ultimate guide, tailored to beginners and seasoned hosts alike.

What You'll Learn

So, what can you expect to learn? Get ready for a deep dive into the nitty-gritty of Airbnb success. From setting your goals and crafting irresistible listings to providing stellar guest experiences and navigating the legal maze, we'll leave no stone unturned.

Setting Expectations

But before we jump into the meaty stuff, let's set some expectations. While Airbnb offers boundless opportunities, it's not a get-rich-quick scheme. Success requires effort, dedication, and a sprinkle of creativity. It's a journey, and like any journey, it starts with a single step.

The Path to Airbnb Success

Throughout this book, we'll guide you along the path to Airbnb success. We'll provide you with practical tips, real-life stories, and expert advice to help you make the most of this incredible platform. Whether you're looking to make a few extra bucks or build a thriving Airbnb empire, we've got you covered.

The Importance of Taking Action

But here's the thing: knowledge alone won't cut it. You need to take action. So, as you dive into the pages ahead, remember that every piece of wisdom you acquire is a step closer to your Airbnb dreams.

The Power of Airbnb Wealth

Now, you might be wondering why this is the perfect time to get started. Well, the answer is simple: Airbnb is on fire!

It's not just a trend; it's a movement that's reshaping the way people travel and experience the world.

Your Role in the Airbnb Ecosystem

And what's your role in this grand ecosystem? You have the potential to be a trailblazer, a host extraordinaire, and a key player in the Airbnb revolution. Your unique property, your warm hospitality, and your commitment to excellence can create ripples of joy for travelers worldwide.

Let's Begin the Journey!

So, are you ready? Are you excited to embark on this thrilling adventure? The pages ahead are filled with insights, strategies, and a sprinkle of humor to keep things lighthearted. We'll share stories of Airbnb hosts who turned their spare spaces into money-making machines and created unforgettable experiences for their guests.

So, grab your favorite beverage, find a comfy chair, and let's dive headfirst into the incredible world of Airbnb. Your journey to financial freedom, unique adventures, and unforgettable moments starts right here, right now. Welcome to the Airbnb Revolution!

Chapter 1:

The Airbnb Revolution: A Paradigm Shift in Real Estate

Imagine a world where the boundaries between traveler and host blur into delightful camaraderie. Where staying in a stranger's home becomes an adventure, not a risk. This is the essence of the Airbnb revolution, a movement that has shaken the foundations of traditional real estate and hospitality.

The Sharing Economy's Impact on Industries

To understand the Airbnb revolution, let's first talk about the sharing economy. It's a buzzworthy term that signifies a fundamental shift in how we consume goods and services. No longer are we content with mere ownership; we want access. And it's this desire for access that has given birth to an array of innovative companies, Airbnb being one of the brightest stars.

The sharing economy has touched nearly every industry, from transportation with Uber to dining with food delivery services like Uber Eats. It's about optimizing resources, reducing waste, and fostering connections between individuals who have something to offer and those who seek it.

Disrupting Traditional Real Estate

Enter Airbnb, the disruptor-in-chief of the traditional real estate and hospitality sector. In the not-so-distant past, if you wanted to book a place to stay while traveling, your options were limited to hotels, motels, and maybe the occasional bed and breakfast. These options came with standardized rooms, corporate decor, and often, a hefty price tag.

But Airbnb took a bold step and turned this model on its head. It unlocked the hidden potential in millions of homes around the world. Suddenly, that spare bedroom or cozy cottage in your backyard could become a desirable destination for travelers. It was a revelation that changed the way we think about real estate and hospitality.

The Birth and Growth of Airbnb

The story of Airbnb's inception is both humble and inspiring. It all began with three friends, Brian Chesky, Joe Gebbia, and Nathan Blecharczyk, who were struggling to pay rent in San Francisco. Facing the prospect of living off cereal and instant noodles, they had an idea. They decided to rent out air mattresses in their living room to attendees of a design conference coming to town. They called it the "Air Bed & Breakfast."

This quirky idea laid the foundation for what would become Airbnb. It started as a way to make ends meet but quickly evolved into something much grander. The concept caught on, and soon, they were offering more than air mattresses. They were providing unique, local experiences that left travelers raving.

The Airbnb Business Model

Airbnb's business model is beautifully simple yet incredibly effective. It acts as a platform that connects hosts with guests. Hosts list their properties, be it a spare room, an entire home, or even a treehouse, and travelers book these spaces for their stay. Airbnb takes a percentage of each booking as a commission, allowing hosts to monetize their spaces and travelers to find affordable, unique accommodations.

This model not only breathed new life into traditional real estate but also fueled a cultural shift in the way we travel. It transformed anonymous hotel stays into personalized, local adventures.

Airbnb's Influence on Travel Trends

Airbnb didn't just disrupt the hospitality industry; it gave rise to entirely new travel trends. Now, travelers aren't merely tourists; they're explorers, adventurers, and temporary locals. Staying in a residential neighborhood, chatting with neighbors, and dining at local eateries became part of the travel experience.

This shift in travel behavior led to the rise of the "experience economy." Travelers sought meaningful connections and authentic encounters, and Airbnb delivered. Suddenly, you could stay in a cozy cottage in the heart of Tuscany, share a meal with a local family in Tokyo, or sleep under the stars in a desert yurt. The possibilities were as diverse as the world itself.

Challenges Faced by Traditional Hospitality

While Airbnb was riding high on its wave of success, traditional hotels and the hospitality industry had to take notice. They faced the reality that their model needed a refresh. It wasn't enough to offer a bed and a minibar; guests wanted a story, a connection, an experience.

The disruptor had laid down the gauntlet, and traditional hospitality had to adapt or risk obsolescence. Hotels started incorporating local experiences, redesigning their spaces, and enhancing guest services to compete with the allure of Airbnb.

How Airbnb Bridges the Gap

So, how does Airbnb bridge the gap between travelers and hosts, you might wonder? It's all about the platform. Airbnb's website and app serve as the digital bridge connecting these two groups. Hosts can create listings with descriptions, photos, and availability calendars, while travelers can search for and book these listings based on their preferences.

The platform provides tools for communication, secure payment processing, and even a review system that builds trust between hosts and guests. It's a seamless experience designed to foster connections and make travel more accessible and enjoyable.

The Global Reach of Airbnb

What began as an air mattress in a living room is now a global phenomenon. Airbnb has spread its wings and landed in over 220 countries and regions, with millions of listings to choose from. It's become a trusted name in travel, with hosts and guests from diverse backgrounds and cultures.

From the bustling streets of New York City to the serene landscapes of New Zealand, Airbnb has made it possible to experience the world in a way that suits your style and budget. The global reach of Airbnb means you can find a place to stay almost anywhere, whether you're embarking on a weekend getaway or a months-long adventure.

The Financial Potential of Airbnb

Now, let's talk about the part that might pique your interest the most: the financial potential of Airbnb. While Airbnb revolutionized the way we travel, it also opened up exciting opportunities for individuals like you. Whether you have a spare room, a vacation home, or an entire apartment building, you can leverage Airbnb to generate income.

Imagine turning your unused spaces into lucrative assets. That spare room that collects dust? It can become a steady stream of rental income. That vacation home you visit once a year? It can pay for itself and then some. Airbnb offers a path to financial freedom, where your property becomes a source of wealth.

The Future of Real Estate and Airbnb

So, what does the future hold for real estate and Airbnb? The trajectory is undeniably upward. Airbnb continues to innovate, introducing new features and services that enhance the hosting and traveling experience. From flexible booking options to enhanced cleaning protocols, Airbnb adapts to meet the changing needs of guests and hosts.

As the sharing economy gains momentum, we can expect to see even more creative ways to monetize assets. It's not just about renting rooms; it's about sharing skills, offering unique experiences, and building connections.

How You Fit into the Airbnb Revolution

Now, you might be wondering, "How do I fit into this Airbnb revolution?" The answer is simple: you are a vital part of it. Whether you're a traveler seeking unique experiences or a property owner looking to monetize your space, you play a role in this transformative movement.

Airbnb empowers individuals to be hosts, to share their stories, their homes, and their cities with the world. It allows travelers to explore the globe with a sense of belonging, to discover the heart of a place through its people.

Building Wealth with Airbnb

As we dive deeper into this book, you'll discover how to harness the power of Airbnb to build wealth, create memorable experiences, and embrace the change that's sweeping the world of real estate and hospitality. So, let's explore how you can embark on this exciting journey of building wealth with Airbnb.

Embracing the Change

Embracing change can be both exhilarating and daunting. But, as they say, "Change is the only constant." Airbnb's disruptive influence on real estate and travel is a prime example of change that opens doors to new possibilities.

Think back to the first time you heard about Airbnb. Perhaps you were skeptical, wondering, "Would people really stay in strangers' homes?" Fast forward to today, and millions of travelers have not only stayed in these unique spaces but have celebrated their experiences.

Embracing the change means acknowledging that traditional norms and business models are evolving. It's about recognizing that the sharing economy, fueled by platforms like Airbnb, has become an integral part of our lives. It's about seizing the opportunities that arise when you adapt to the changing landscape.

Taking Advantage of the Opportunity

Now, let's talk about seizing opportunities. Airbnb presents an extraordinary opportunity for you to not only enhance your travel experiences but also to create financial stability and wealth. The possibilities are as vast and varied as the listings you'll find on the platform.

As a traveler, Airbnb opens the door to immersive and authentic experiences. It allows you to connect with local hosts who offer insights into their culture, their favorite spots, and their way of life. It lets you explore the world on your terms, in spaces that resonate with your preferences and budget.

For hosts, Airbnb offers a chance to transform underutilized spaces into income-generating assets. Whether you have a spare room, an entire property, or a unique niche accommodation, you have the potential to earn substantial income. This income can support your financial goals, fund your dream vacations, or even serve as a primary source of revenue.

But seizing this opportunity requires knowledge, strategy, and a dash of entrepreneurial spirit. It involves understanding the platform, setting realistic goals, and delivering exceptional experiences to your guests. In the pages ahead, we'll delve into the nuts and bolts of building wealth with Airbnb, equipping you with the tools and insights you need to succeed.

The Airbnb Millionaire Manifesto

This book isn't just a guide; it's your roadmap to Airbnb success. We've named it "The Airbnb Millionaire Manifesto" because it embodies the principles, strategies, and mindset that can elevate you to the status of an Airbnb millionaire. While the title may evoke images of luxury and extravagance, being an Airbnb millionaire is about more than just money.

It's about the freedom to live life on your terms, to explore the world, and to create memorable experiences for yourself and others. It's about breaking free from the constraints of traditional thinking and embracing a new way of living and earning. It's about discovering the potential within you and your property, whether it's a cozy apartment, a charming cottage, or a unique and offbeat space.

Throughout the chapters that follow, we'll unravel the secrets to maximizing your Airbnb earnings, creating unforgettable guest experiences, and navigating the challenges that may arise along the way. We'll share stories of hosts who have turned their properties into thriving businesses and guests who have embarked on life-changing adventures through Airbnb.

Your Role in the Airbnb Community

As you dive into the world of Airbnb, you're not just joining a platform; you're becoming a part of a global community.

Airbnb is a network of hosts and travelers, each with their stories to tell, their spaces to share, and their dreams to pursue. It's a community built on trust, hospitality, and the belief that the world is a better place when we open our doors and hearts to one another.

Your role in this community is unique and valuable. As a host, you become an ambassador for your city, offering travelers a glimpse into the local way of life. You become a creator of memories, providing guests with experiences they'll cherish for a lifetime. As a traveler, you become a global citizen, connecting with people from diverse backgrounds and cultures.

The Airbnb community is a diverse tapestry of stories, and we're excited to add your chapter to it. Whether you're just starting or you're an experienced host looking to up your game, you have a role to play in shaping the future of travel and hospitality.

The End is Just the Beginning

As we conclude this chapter, remember that the end of one journey is merely the beginning of another. You've taken the first step toward understanding the Airbnb revolution and its potential to transform your life. The adventure ahead is filled with insights, strategies, and a few surprises along the way.

So, fasten your seatbelt and prepare for an exciting ride through the world of Airbnb. The next chapters will equip you with the knowledge and tools you need to embark on your path to Airbnb success. Whether you're seeking financial freedom, unforgettable experiences, or a blend of both, the Airbnb Millionaire Manifesto is your trusted companion on this journey.

The future is bright, the possibilities are limitless, and your adventure begins now. Welcome to the Airbnb revolution, where your dreams and Airbnb's platform converge to create a world of opportunities. Get ready to unlock the secrets of Airbnb wealth and make your mark in this transformative landscape.

Chapter 2:

Setting Your Goals: Defining Your Path to Airbnb Success

Welcome to the next step on your journey to Airbnb success, where we'll dive into the art and science of goal setting. As the saying goes, "If you aim at nothing, you'll hit it every time." In this chapter, we'll equip you with the tools and strategies to aim high and hit the mark in your Airbnb venture.

The Power of Goal Setting

Goal setting is a superpower that can propel you toward success in any endeavor, including your Airbnb hosting journey. It's the act of defining what you want to achieve and creating a roadmap to get there. Setting clear and inspiring goals gives your actions purpose and direction.

Think of your goals as the North Star guiding your ship through the vast ocean of possibilities. They provide focus, motivation, and a sense of accomplishment as you reach each milestone. Without goals, it's like embarking on a road trip without a map or destination in mind—you might enjoy the journey, but you're unlikely to reach your desired endpoint.

The Connection Between Goals and Motivation

Goals and motivation are inseparable companions on your journey to Airbnb success. Your goals are like the carrots dangling in front of the proverbial donkey, urging you forward with each step. They serve as a source of inspiration, reminding you why you embarked on this adventure in the first place.

Imagine this: You set a goal to achieve Superhost status on Airbnb, a prestigious badge of honor that comes with perks like increased visibility and trust among guests. The thought of earning that title fuels your motivation to go the extra mile in providing exceptional guest experiences.

Short-Term vs. Long-Term Goals

Now, let's talk about the time dimension of goals. Goals come in two main flavors: short-term and long-term. Short-term goals are like bite-sized snacks along the way, providing quick bursts of satisfaction as you achieve them. They could be as simple as receiving your first five-star review or earning your first $500 in Airbnb income.

Long-term goals, on the other hand, are the grand visions that guide your journey over the horizon. They might include becoming an Airbnb Superhost, generating a specific monthly income from your listings, or even acquiring additional properties for Airbnb hosting.

The secret to successful goal setting lies in finding the right balance between short-term and long-term goals. Short-term goals keep you motivated with regular doses of achievement, while long-term goals provide the overarching direction and purpose.

Specific, Measurable, Achievable, Relevant, and Time-Bound (SMART) Goals

You may have heard of SMART goals before, and there's a reason they're popular—they work! SMART stands for

Specific, Measurable, Achievable, Relevant, and Time-Bound. Let's break down each element:

1.   **Specific**: Your goal should be crystal clear and specific. Instead of saying, "I want to make money on Airbnb," specify, "I want to earn $5,000 per month through Airbnb hosting."

2.   **Measurable:** Goals should be quantifiable so you can track your progress. In our example, you can measure your success by your monthly earnings.

3.   **Achievable:** Goals should be realistic and attainable. While dreaming big is encouraged, ensure your goals are within reach. If you're just starting, aiming for $10,000 in monthly income might not be achievable right away.

4.   **Relevant:** Your goals should align with your aspirations and values. If financial freedom and travel adventures are your passions, an Airbnb-related goal is highly relevant.

5.   **Time-Bound:** Attach a timeframe to your goals. Instead of saying, "I want to earn $5,000 per month," say, "I want to earn $5,000 per month within one year."

Applying the SMART criteria to your Airbnb goals makes them concrete, actionable, and less daunting.

Identifying Your Core Motivations

Before you set your Airbnb goals, take a moment to explore your core motivations. Understanding why you're venturing into Airbnb hosting will not only help you set more meaningful goals but also keep you motivated during challenging times.

Your motivations might range from financial freedom and supporting your family to a deep passion for hospitality and creating memorable guest experiences. Perhaps you're motivated by the desire to travel more or to convert your idle property into a source of income.

Take a moment to jot down your motivations. These will serve as the fuel that propels you forward on your Airbnb journey.

Visualizing Your Ideal Airbnb Journey

Close your eyes and picture your ideal Airbnb journey. What does it look like? Where are your listings located? How do you interact with your guests? How does hosting on Airbnb fit into your life and your broader aspirations?

Visualization is a powerful tool for goal setting. It creates a mental blueprint of your desired future, making your goals feel more achievable and real. It also helps you clarify your vision and align your goals with the lifestyle you want to create.

Crafting Your Personal Airbnb Vision Statement

Now that you've visualized your ideal Airbnb journey, it's time to distill it into a concise vision statement. This statement will serve as a guiding light, reminding you of your overarching purpose and aspirations as an Airbnb host.

Your vision statement can be as simple as: "To create unforgettable guest experiences in my unique properties, enabling me to achieve financial freedom and explore the world on my terms."

Crafting your vision statement is a personal and introspective process. It's a declaration of your intentions and a source of inspiration on your hosting journey.

Aligning Your Goals with Your Values

As you set your Airbnb goals, it's crucial to ensure they align with your core values. Your values are the principles that define what's important to you in life. They act as a compass, guiding your decisions and actions.

For instance, if one of your core values is sustainability, your Airbnb goals might include implementing eco-friendly practices in your listings and promoting responsible tourism. If family is a top value, your goals might prioritize a flexible hosting schedule that allows quality time with loved ones.

Aligning your goals with your values ensures that your pursuit of Airbnb success is not only financially rewarding but also personally fulfilling.

Setting Realistic Milestones

Goals can be overwhelming when viewed as a massive mountain to climb. To make them more manageable, break them down into realistic milestones. These are the smaller, actionable steps that lead you toward your larger goals.

For example, if your long-term goal is to become an Airbnb Superhost, your milestones might include:

- Receiving your first five-star review

- Achieving a 90% or higher response rate to guest inquiries

- Earning Superhost status

- Enhancing the decor and amenities of your listing

- Hosting a certain number of guests per month

These milestones serve as stepping stones to your ultimate goal and provide a sense of achievement along the way.

Breaking Down Goals into Actionable Steps

With your milestones in mind, it's time to break down your goals into actionable steps. These are the specific actions you need to take to reach each milestone. Let's take the example of achieving Superhost status:

1. **Improve Guest Communication:** Set a goal to respond to guest inquiries within a few hours and provide informative, friendly responses.

2. **Enhance Your Listing:** Identify areas for improvement in your listing, such as updating photos, adding more amenities, or enhancing the cleanliness and comfort of your space.

3. **Optimize Pricing:** Research comparable listings in your area and adjust your pricing to remain competitive and attract more bookings.

4. **Offer Exceptional Experiences:** Create a guidebook or welcome kit for guests, recommending local attractions, restaurants, and activities.

5. **Achieve High Ratings:** Continuously strive to provide excellent guest experiences to earn consistently high ratings and reviews.

Breaking down your goals into actionable steps not only makes them less intimidating but also provides a clear roadmap for your journey.

The Importance of Flexibility

While setting goals is crucial, it's equally important to remain flexible. Life is unpredictable, and unexpected challenges and opportunities may arise along your Airbnb journey. Flexibility allows you to adapt your goals and strategies as needed.

For instance, if a global pandemic disrupts travel patterns, you might need to adjust your goals to focus on local and long-term bookings rather than short-term tourism. Flexibility ensures that setbacks don't discourage you but instead prompt you to find creative solutions.

Tracking Progress and Celebrating Achievements

As you embark on your Airbnb journey, track your progress toward your goals. Use tools like spreadsheets or goal tracking apps to monitor your milestones and the steps you've completed. Regularly reviewing your progress keeps you accountable and motivated.

Additionally, celebrate your achievements along the way. Every milestone reached, no matter how small, is a cause for celebration. Treat yourself to a favorite meal, plan a mini-vacation, or simply take a moment to acknowledge your hard work and dedication.

Overcoming Obstacles and Challenges

It's important to recognize that obstacles and challenges are a natural part of any journey, including your Airbnb hosting adventure. These hurdles can range from guest issues and property maintenance to economic downturns and regulatory changes.

The key to overcoming obstacles is resilience. When faced with challenges, view them as opportunities to learn and grow. Seek support from Airbnb host communities, fellow hosts, or online forums where experienced hosts share their wisdom and advice.

Revising and Refining Your Goals

As your Airbnb journey unfolds, you may find that your initial goals need adjustment. Perhaps you've achieved a milestone ahead of schedule and need to set a new one, or maybe changes in your life require you to revise your long-term goals.

This flexibility is essential for staying motivated and aligned with your evolving aspirations. Remember that goals are not set in stone; they can and should adapt to your circumstances and ambitions.

Staying Committed to Your Airbnb Goals

Setting goals is just the beginning; staying committed to them is the ongoing challenge. To maintain your commitment:

1.   **Review Regularly:** Schedule regular check-ins with your goals to assess your progress and make any necessary adjustments.

2.   Stay Inspired: Keep your vision statement visible, whether it's a framed print, a screensaver, or a handwritten note. It serves as a constant reminder of your purpose.

3.   Find an Accountability Partner: Share your goals with a friend, family member, or fellow host who can provide encouragement and hold you accountable.

4.   Stay Informed: Stay updated on Airbnb trends, best practices, and new features to remain competitive and informed.

5.Celebrate Milestones: Celebrate not only the achievement of major goals but also the completion of smaller milestones. Recognize your efforts.

With these strategies in place, you'll be well-equipped to set, pursue, and achieve your Airbnb goals. Remember that your journey is unique, and your goals should reflect your individual aspirations and values.

In the chapters ahead, we'll explore specific goals and strategies for maximizing your success on Airbnb. Whether you're focused on financial milestones, guest satisfaction, or a combination of both, we'll provide the guidance you need to thrive in the world of Airbnb hosting. Your adventure continues, and your goals are the compass that will guide you to success.

Chapter 3:

Creating Your Airbnb Strategy: From Listings to Guests

Welcome to the heart of your Airbnb journey, where we dive deep into creating a winning strategy that will make your hosting venture a resounding success. This chapter is like the blueprint for your Airbnb adventure, helping you navigate the intricacies of the platform and leave a lasting impression on your guests.

Understanding the Airbnb Ecosystem

Before we delve into strategy, let's understand the Airbnb ecosystem. Airbnb operates as a two-sided marketplace, connecting hosts with travelers. Hosts provide accommodations, while travelers seek unique and affordable places to stay. This ecosystem thrives on trust, hospitality, and the sense of belonging.

As a host, you're a crucial part of this ecosystem. Your role is to create a welcoming space, offer outstanding experiences, and showcase the local flavor of your area. In return, you have the opportunity to earn income, meet fascinating people, and even transform your property into a thriving business.

Exploring Different Hosting Styles

One of the fascinating aspects of Airbnb hosting is that it can take various forms, depending on your preferences and circumstances. Let's explore a few hosting styles:

1.   **Private Room:** You share your home with guests while maintaining your privacy. Ideal if you have extra bedrooms.

2.   **Entire Place:** You rent out your entire property, be it a house, apartment, or even a unique space like a treehouse.

3.   **Vacation Rental:** You may own a second home or investment property exclusively for Airbnb rentals.

4.   **Co-hosting:** You assist other hosts in managing their listings for a fee.

5.   **Experience Host:** Beyond accommodations, you offer unique experiences to travelers, like guided tours, cooking classes, or outdoor adventures.

Your hosting style should align with your property type, resources, and personal preferences.

Assessing Your Resources and Capabilities

Hosting on Airbnb requires an investment of time, effort, and resources. Before you dive in, assess what you can realistically commit to your hosting venture. Consider factors like:

-    **Time:** How much time can you dedicate to guest communication, check-ins, cleanings, and maintenance?

-    **Space:** What type of property do you have, and how can you optimize it for guests?

-    **Budget:** Determine your hosting budget for essentials like cleaning, amenities, and decor.

-      **Skills:** Identify any skills or talents you can leverage, such as photography, interior design, or cooking.

-      **Support:** Do you need assistance with tasks like cleaning or guest communication?

By understanding your resources and capabilities, you can set clear expectations and tailor your strategy accordingly.

The Importance of Market Research

Market research is your secret weapon in the Airbnb world. It involves studying your local market to understand demand, pricing trends, and competitor listings. Here's how to get started:

1.   **Study Local Listings:** Explore Airbnb listings in your area. Pay attention to their prices, amenities, and reviews.

2.   **Identify Trends**: Look for trends in guest preferences. Are travelers seeking pet-friendly spaces, homes with outdoor amenities, or unique, themed properties?

3.   **Pricing Analysis:** Analyze the pricing of similar listings. Consider factors like location, size, and features.

4.   **Seasonal Demand:** Understand the seasonal peaks and lows in your area. Adjust your pricing accordingly.

5.   **Guest Reviews:** Read guest reviews to understand what travelers appreciate and areas where hosts can improve.

Market research arms you with valuable insights to finetune your strategy and gain a competitive edge.

Identifying Your Target Audience

Just as a chef tailors a dish to suit a specific palate, you should tailor your Airbnb strategy to attract your ideal guests. Start by identifying your target audience:

Business Travelers: Ideal for urban listings with convenient access to business hubs.

- **Families:** Consider family-friendly amenities and spacious properties.

- **Couples:** Focus on cozy, romantic settings.

- **Adventure Seekers:** Highlight nearby outdoor activities and adventures.

- **Cultural Explorers:** Emphasize the local culture, history, and cuisine.

Understanding your target audience helps you craft listings and experiences that resonate with their preferences.

Tailoring Your Strategy to Your Property Type

Each property type comes with its unique hosting opportunities and challenges. Let's explore how to tailor your strategy to different property types:

1. **Private Room:** Emphasize the welcoming atmosphere and personal interaction with guests.

2. **Entire Place:** Highlight the privacy, convenience, and unique features of your property.

3. **Vacation Rental:** Offer the allure of a home away from home, with a focus on relaxation and recreation.

4.   Experience Host: Create captivating experiences that align with your local area and personal passions.

Understanding your property type allows you to optimize your strategy for maximum success.

The Art of Crafting Compelling Listings

Your Airbnb listing is like the cover of a book—it should entice travelers to learn more about your property. Crafting a compelling listing is an art form that involves several key elements:

Tips for Writing Irresistible Descriptions

-    **Be Descriptive:** Paint a vivid picture with your words. Describe the ambiance, style, and atmosphere of your space.

-    **Highlight Unique Features:** What sets your property apart? Whether it's a cozy fireplace, a breathtaking view, or a private garden, make it shine.

-    **Use Positive Language:** Use positive and inviting language to create excitement. Instead of saying "small," say "cozy."

-    **Tell a Story:** Share the story of your property and its history, if applicable. It adds personality and charm.

-    **Be Honest:** Honesty builds trust. Accurately represent your property, and mention any potential quirks or limitations.

Optimizing Your Listing Title

Your listing title is the first thing potential guests see, so make it count. A great title should:

- **Be Specific:** Mention the type of property, unique features, and location.

  Include Keywords: Use relevant keywords travelers might search for, like "beachfront," "luxury," or "historic district."

- **Evoke Emotion:** Create an emotional connection or curiosity. For example, "Charming Cottage Retreat by the Sea" invokes a sense of relaxation and charm.

Showcasing Your Property's Unique Features Highlight

what makes your property special:

- **Photography:** High-quality photos are worth their weight in gold. Show your space in its best light, both inside and out.

- **Amenities:** List amenities that set your property apart, whether it's a hot tub, a fully equipped kitchen, or a gaming room.

- **Local Attractions:** Mention nearby attractions, restaurants, and activities to entice travelers.

Pricing Strategies for Maximum Profit

Pricing is both an art and a science. It involves finding the sweet spot that attracts guests while maximizing your earnings. Consider these pricing strategies:

- **Competitive Pricing:** Set your prices in line with similar listings in your area.

- **Dynamic Pricing:** Use dynamic pricing tools to adjust rates based on demand, seasons, and local events.

- **Special Offers:** Attract bookings with occasional discounts or special offers.

  Length of Stay Discounts: Offer lower nightly rates for longer stays to encourage extended bookings.

Remember that pricing is not static; it's a dynamic aspect of your strategy that should adapt to market changes.

Adjusting Rates for Seasonal Peaks

Seasonal demand can significantly impact your earnings. Adjust your rates to capitalize on peak seasons and maximize your revenue:

- **High Season:** During peak tourist seasons, like summer at a beach destination, raise your rates to reflect the high demand.

- **Low Season:** In slower months, consider offering lower rates or special deals to attract off-season travelers.

- **Local Events:** If your area hosts major events like festivals or conferences, adjust your rates accordingly.

- **Holidays:** Raise your rates for popular holidays when many travelers are looking for accommodations.

By strategically adjusting your rates throughout the year, you can optimize your income.

Analyzing Competitor Listings

Studying your competition can provide valuable insights into what works and what doesn't in your market. Here's how to analyze competitor listings effectively:

- **Pricing Comparison:** Compare your rates with similar listings. Are you competitively priced?

Amenities: Note the amenities your competitors offer. Are there any gaps you can fill?

- **Guest Reviews:** Read reviews of competing listings to learn what guests appreciate and areas where hosts excel.

- **Availability:** Check the availability of nearby listings to identify potential gaps in the market.

Competitor analysis helps you position your listing more effectively and identify opportunities for improvement.

The Guest Experience: Going Above and Beyond

Now, let's talk about the cherry on top—the guest experience. Providing an exceptional experience not only leads to positive reviews but also encourages repeat bookings and referrals.

Here's how to go above and beyond:

- **Communication:** Be responsive and attentive to guest inquiries and needs.

- **Personalization:** Tailor your interactions and recommendations to each guest's preferences.

- **Cleanliness:** Maintain a spotless space to ensure guests feel comfortable and safe.

- **Amenities:** Consider providing thoughtful extras like snacks, toiletries, or local treats.

- **Local Insights:** Share insider tips on the best local restaurants, attractions, and activities.

- **Check-In Experience**: Make the check-in process seamless and stress-free.

Guest Privacy: Respect your guests' privacy while remaining available for assistance.

- **Feedback:** Encourage guests to leave feedback, and use it to continuously improve.

Remember that exceptional guest experiences lead to rave reviews, which, in turn, boost your listing's visibility and appeal.

In the world of Airbnb, your strategy is your compass, guiding you through the ever-evolving landscape of hosting. By understanding the Airbnb ecosystem, researching your market, and tailoring your approach to your property type and target audience, you'll set the stage for success. Crafting compelling listings and optimizing your pricing ensures you stand out, while an exceptional guest experience leaves a lasting impression.

As you continue your Airbnb journey, keep in mind that success on the platform is a dynamic process. Stay open to learning, adapt your strategy when necessary, and always aim to exceed guest expectations. Your strategy is not a rigid plan but a living document that evolves with your experience and insights.

Chapter 4:

Crafting Irresistible Airbnb Listings

Welcome to the art of crafting Airbnb listings that beckon travelers to your doorstep like a siren's call. Think of your listing as the first impression, the enticing aroma wafting from a bakery that draws passersby inside. In this chapter, we'll unveil the secrets of creating listings so irresistible that guests can't resist clicking that "Book Now" button.

The Art of Writing Compelling Descriptions

Writing compelling descriptions for your Airbnb listing is akin to penning a captivating story, one that transports potential guests into a world of possibilities. Here's how to weave the magic:

Consider your property as the protagonist, and paint a vivid picture. Describe its style, character, and unique charm. Is it a cozy cabin nestled in the woods, a chic urban apartment, or a historic home with a story to tell?

Tips for Eye-Catching Titles

Your listing title is the first thing guests see, and first impressions matter. Think of it as the marquee of a Broadway show, beckoning people to buy a ticket. Here are tips for crafting an eye-catching title:

Be Specific: Mention your property type, key features, and location.

Evoke Emotion: Create a sense of desire or curiosity. Instead of "Cozy Studio," try "Charming Studio Retreat in the Heart of the City."

Use Keywords: Incorporate relevant keywords that travelers might use in their searches.

- **Highlight Unique Features:** If your property has a hot tub, a fireplace, or a stunning view, make it known in the title.

Highlighting Your Property's Unique Features

Imagine your property as a treasure chest filled with unique gems. Highlight these gems in your listing description:

- **Amenities:** Mention any special amenities, like a fully equipped kitchen, a private pool, or a garden oasis.

- **Special Touches:** Share unique features that set your property apart, such as a collection of vintage records, a cozy reading nook, or a rooftop terrace with skyline views.

- **Location Perks:** Highlight nearby attractions, restaurants, or events that make your property's location special.

Using Persuasive Language to Attract Guests

Persuasive language is your ally in convincing potential guests that your listing is the ideal choice. Use words that evoke emotion and desire:

- **Inviting:** Describe your space as inviting and welcoming.

- **Luxurious:** Even if your property isn't ultra-luxurious, you can use this term to imply comfort and elegance.

- **Cozy:** Cozy doesn't mean small; it signifies warmth and comfort.

  Spacious: Use this term to create a sense of openness and room to breathe.

Showcasing Your Property's Benefits

Your listing should be like a menu of delightful experiences. Explain how staying at your property benefits guests:

- **Convenience**: Highlight how convenient your location is, whether it's near public transportation, attractions, or restaurants.

- **Comfort:** Emphasize the comfortable amenities that await guests, like a plush mattress, a rainfall shower, or a fully stocked kitchen.

- **Privacy:** Describe how your property offers a private and serene escape from the world.

Crafting a Memorable Introduction

The introduction of your listing is like the opening scene of a movie—it sets the tone and captivates your audience. Make it memorable by:

- **Telling a Story:** Share the story of your property, its history, or the experiences guests can look forward to.

- **Engaging Descriptions:** Use engaging language that sparks curiosity and draws readers in.

- **Personal Connection:** Express your excitement to host and create connections with travelers.

Describing Each Room in Detail

Think of each room description as a preview of what guests will experience. Take them on a virtual tour:

Living Room: Describe the ambiance, seating arrangements, and any entertainment options like a TV or board games.

- **Bedrooms:** Highlight the comfort of the beds, the quality of linens, and any unique features like a walk-in closet or a balcony.

- **Kitchen:** Detail the kitchen's equipment, appliances, and any special touches like a coffee bar or a breakfast nook.

- **Bathroom:** Mention the bathroom's amenities, cleanliness, and any spa-like features such as a soaking tub or a rain shower.

Creating a Sense of Ambiance and Atmosphere

Transport your guests into the world you've created within your property:

- **Use Descriptive Words:** Paint a picture with words, describing the soft glow of dimmed lights, the aroma of freshly brewed coffee, or the sound of a crackling fireplace.

- **Mood Setting:** Share how your space sets the mood for relaxation, romance, or adventure, depending on your target audience.

Utilizing Keywords for Search Optimization

Keywords are the secret sauce that helps travelers discover your listing. Incorporate relevant keywords that travelers might use in their searches. Think about what sets your property apart and include those unique features.

Formatting and Organization of Your Listing

A well-organized listing is like a well-arranged bouquet—it's visually appealing and easy to navigate:

- **Bullet Points:** Use bullet points to highlight key features, amenities, and benefits.

- **Subheadings:** Organize your description with subheadings for each section, such as "Bedroom," "Kitchen," "Amenities," and "Location."

- **Whitespace:** Ensure your listing is easy on the eyes by incorporating whitespace between paragraphs and sections.

- **Lists:** Use numbered or bulleted lists to make important information stand out.

A well-organized listing not only makes it easier for guests to find the information they need but also adds a professional touch to your presentation.

The Importance of Honesty and Transparency

Honesty is the cornerstone of a successful Airbnb listing. Transparency builds trust with potential guests and sets realistic expectations. Here's how to maintain honesty and transparency:

- **Accurate Photos:** Ensure your photos accurately represent your property. Use high-quality images and avoid over-editing.

- **Clear Policies:** Be upfront about your house rules, check-in and check-out times, and any additional fees.

  Property Condition: If your property has quirks or minor imperfections, mention them. Honesty fosters goodwill, and guests appreciate straightforwardness.

- **Cancellation Policy:** Clearly state your cancellation policy, whether it's flexible, moderate, or strict.

By being honest and transparent, you'll attract guests who are the right fit for your property and reduce the likelihood of misunderstandings.

Avoiding Common Listing Mistakes

While crafting your listing, be aware of common pitfalls that can deter potential guests:

- **Incomplete Information**: Ensure you've filled out all the necessary details in your listing, from the number of bedrooms to the pricing.

- **Spelling and Grammar Errors:** Proofread your description to avoid spelling and grammar mistakes that can detract from your professionalism.

- **Generic Language**: Avoid using generic phrases like "cozy" or "great location" without providing specific details.

- **Overhyping:** While it's essential to highlight your property's strengths, avoid exaggerations that can lead to disappointed guests.

- **Neglecting Mobile Optimization:** Many travelers browse and book on mobile devices, so ensure your listing is mobile-friendly.

Updating and Refreshing Your Listing

Your listing isn't set in stone; it's a dynamic document that can evolve over time. To keep it fresh and appealing:

- **Seasonal Updates**: Update your description to reflect seasonal changes, events, and local attractions.

- **New Amenities:** If you add new amenities or features to your property, be sure to mention them.

- **Guest Feedback:** Pay attention to guest feedback and use it to make improvements.

- **Professional Photos:** Periodically invest in professional photography to keep your images current and enticing.

Leveraging Guest Reviews for Improvement

Guest reviews are a goldmine of insights. Pay attention to both positive and negative feedback:

- **Positive Reviews:** Use them to highlight what guests love about your property in your listing.

- **Negative Reviews:** Address any concerns or issues raised by previous guests and demonstrate how you've resolved them.

Your ability to listen to guests and continuously improve your property based on their feedback can set you apart as a host.

Evolving Your Listing Over Time

The Airbnb landscape is ever-evolving, and so should your listing. Keep an eye on industry trends, competitive listings, and changes in traveler preferences. Stay open to adapting your listing strategy to remain competitive and appealing.

In the dynamic world of Airbnb, crafting irresistible listings is an art form that combines creativity, marketing savvy, and a deep understanding of your property and target audience. Remember that your listing is your property's online persona, and it should shine as brightly as your real-world space. By embracing the techniques and tips outlined in this chapter, you'll be well on your way to creating listings that beckon travelers to experience the magic of your property. So, pick up your virtual pen and let your listing come to life, one word at a time.

Chapter 5:

Stunning Photography: Capturing Your Property's Best Angle

Welcome to the dazzling world of Airbnb photography, where a picture is worth not just a thousand words but also a thousand bookings. In this chapter, we'll explore how the art of photography can elevate your Airbnb listing to new heights, enticing travelers with the promise of a memorable stay.

The Importance of Visual Appeal in Listings

Imagine your Airbnb listing as a virtual open house, where potential guests stroll through your property from the comfort of their screens. In this digital age, visual appeal reigns supreme. Studies have shown that properties with high-quality photos receive more bookings and command higher nightly rates.

Pictures provide a first impression, and a positive one can be the difference between a guest choosing your property or scrolling past it. To make your listing stand out, it's crucial to master the art of photography.

DIY Photography Tips for Hosts

You don't need to be a professional photographer to capture stunning images of your property. With some basic skills and the right techniques, you can create a visual masterpiece:

Choosing the Right Lighting and Time of Day

- **Natural Light:** Whenever possible, rely on natural light to illuminate your space. Soft, diffused light is flattering and creates a warm ambiance.

- **Golden Hour:** Photograph during the golden hours of sunrise and sunset for a magical, soft glow.

- **Avoid Harsh Shadows:** Harsh midday sunlight can create unappealing shadows. If you must shoot during this time, use curtains or blinds to diffuse the light.

Using High-Quality Camera Equipment

While smartphones can take decent photos, investing in a good camera can significantly improve your photography. Here are some camera tips:

- **DSLR or Mirrorless Camera:** Consider using a DSLR or mirrorless camera for greater control over settings and image quality.

- **Tripod**: A stable platform ensures sharp images, especially in low light.

- **Wide-Angle Lens:** A wide-angle lens can capture more of your space, making it feel more spacious.

Composition and Framing Techniques

The way you compose and frame your shots can make a world of difference:

- **Rule of Thirds:** Imagine your frame divided into a grid of nine squares. Place key elements along these lines or intersections.

- **Leading Lines:** Use natural lines or objects in your space to draw the viewer's eye to the focal point.

- **Symmetry:** Showcase symmetry if your space has it. It's visually pleasing and gives a sense of balance.

Capturing Key Features and Amenities Highlight

what sets your property apart:

- **Amenities:** Showcase amenities like a luxurious bathtub, a cozy fireplace, or a fully equipped kitchen.

- **Unique Features:** Capture the uniqueness of your space, whether it's a breathtaking view, a charming window seat, or a quirky piece of art.

- **Room Flow**: Show how the different rooms in your property connect and flow together.

Enhancing Your Photos with Editing

Editing is like the final touch of a skilled chef—it elevates your dish from good to extraordinary. Consider these editing tips:

- **Consistency:** Maintain a consistent style for all your photos, whether it's vibrant and colorful or muted and cozy.

- **Brightness and Contrast:** Adjust brightness and contrast to ensure your photos pop without looking overexposed.

- **Color Correction**: Correct any color casts that may result from artificial lighting.

- **Crop and Straighten**: Crop and straighten your photos to ensure they're well-framed and free of distractions.

- **Remove Clutter**: Edit out any visual clutter or personal items that could distract from the property itself.

Creating a Consistent Visual Style

Consistency in your photos helps create a memorable brand for your property:

- **Color Palette:** Use a consistent color palette in your decor and photography.

- **Furniture Arrangement:** Keep furniture arrangements and decorations consistent to avoid confusion for guests.

The Power of Before-and-After Photos

Before-and-after photos can be a powerful storytelling tool. They showcase the transformation of your property:

- **Renovations:** Show the progress and improvements made to your property.

- **Seasonal Changes:** Highlight how your property changes with the seasons.

Hiring Professional Photographers

If photography isn't your forte or you want to take your listing to the next level, consider hiring a professional photographer:

- **Experience:** Professional photographers have the skills and equipment to capture your property at its best.

- **Time-Saving:** Hiring a pro saves you time and effort, allowing you to focus on other aspects of hosting.

- **Higher Booking Rates:** Properties with professional photos tend to command higher nightly rates and receive more bookings.

Showcasing the Neighborhood and Surroundings

Your property isn't just the physical space; it's also about the neighborhood and surroundings:

- **Local Attractions:** Include photos of nearby attractions, parks, restaurants, and shops to give guests a sense of what's around.

- **Scenic Views:** If your property offers stunning views, be sure to capture them.

Keeping Your Photo Gallery Fresh

Don't let your photo gallery become stale. Keep it updated:

- **Seasonal Refresh:** Update photos to reflect different seasons or holidays.

- **Renovations:** If you make improvements or changes, update your photos to reflect the new look.

- **Professional Checkup:** Consider getting professional photos taken regularly to keep your listing looking its best.

The Role of Videos in Listings

Videos are the new frontier in Airbnb photography:

- **Virtual Tours:** Create virtual tours of your property to give potential guests a more immersive experience.

- **Host Introductions:** Consider including a short video where you introduce yourself as the host.

Managing Guest Expectations through Photos Your photos should set clear expectations:

- **Accurate Representation:** Ensure your photos accurately represent your property to avoid disappointment upon arrival.

- **Show What's Included:** Showcase amenities and features that are included in the booking.

- **Emphasize Unique Features:** Highlight any unique or standout features that make your property special.

Maintaining a Portfolio of Property Images

As a host, you should have a portfolio of property images:

- **High-Quality Portfolio**: Collect high-quality images of your property from various angles and perspectives.

- **Backup Photos:** Store backup photos in case you need to update your listing or respond to inquiries.

In the world of Airbnb, stunning photography is your secret weapon. It's the art of telling a visual story that inspires wanderlust and captures the hearts of potential guests. With the tips and techniques outlined in this chapter, you'll transform your property into a visual masterpiece that travelers can't resist. So, grab your camera, set the stage, and let your property shine in the spotlight—it's showtime on Airbnb!

Chapter 6:

Pricing Strategies: Optimizing Rates for Maximum Profit

Welcome to the ever-evolving world of Airbnb pricing—a realm where setting the right rates can mean the difference between a thriving Airbnb venture and one that's merely surviving. In this chapter, we'll embark on a journey through the art and science of pricing your property for maximum profit, all while keeping your guests and the ever-elusive market dynamics in mind.

The Dynamic Nature of Airbnb Pricing

Think of Airbnb pricing as a symphony that constantly plays to a changing audience. It's not a static number but a dynamic dance that adapts to various factors, both internal and external.

The dynamic nature of Airbnb pricing means that it's not a one-size-fits-all equation. Instead, it's a delicate balance between offering value to guests and maximizing your profit potential.

Factors Influencing Pricing Decisions

Before we dive into the intricacies of setting your rates, let's understand the key factors that influence your pricing decisions:

Understanding Your Property's Value

The first step in pricing is understanding the value your property brings to the table. Consider factors like:

Location: Proximity to attractions, transport, and amenities.

- **Amenities:** What unique features or amenities does your property offer?

- **Seasonality:** How does demand change throughout the year?

- **Market Conditions**: Is the market competitive, or are you in a niche?

- **Property Size:** Larger properties generally command higher rates.

Setting Base Rates and Seasonal Adjustments

Every property has its baseline value, and that's where you should start:

- **Base Rate**: Your standard rate for regular days.

- **Seasonal Adjustments**: Modify your rates based on high and low seasons. Raise prices during peak times and offer discounts during slower periods.

The Importance of Competitive Analysis

In the world of Airbnb, your competitors are your allies in pricing strategy. Take the time to analyze similar listings in your area:

- **Compare Rates:** How do your rates stack up against similar properties?

- **Amenities:** Are there amenities or features you offer that others don't?

- **Reviews:** How does your property's reputation compare?

  Occupancy: What occupancy rates do competing listings achieve?

Competitive analysis helps you position your property effectively and understand what guests are willing to pay for similar experiences.

Monitoring Demand and Supply Trends

Like any market, the Airbnb landscape has trends and fluctuations:

- **Special Events**: Prices may surge during major events or conferences in your area.

- **Local Holidays**. Expect increased demand during holidays and long weekends.

- **Low Seasons**: Be prepared to offer competitive rates during off-peak times.

Utilizing Airbnb's Smart Pricing Tool

Airbnb offers a Smart Pricing tool that automates rate adjustments based on demand and supply trends. While it can be a helpful starting point, it's essential to fine-tune the settings to align with your pricing strategy. Don't rely solely on automation; use it as a tool to inform your decisions.

Strategic Use of Minimum and Maximum Stays

Setting minimum and maximum stay requirements can help you achieve your hosting goals:

- **Minimum Stay**: Encourage longer bookings during high demand periods by setting a minimum stay.

  Maximum Stay: Prevent extended stays that might disrupt your availability.

Implementing Length-of-Stay Discounts Encourage

longer stays with tiered pricing:

- Offer a discount for stays of a week or more.

- Consider deeper discounts for month-long bookings.

Length-of-stay discounts can attract guests looking for extended stays, boosting your occupancy.

Adjusting Rates for Special Events and Holidays

Don't miss out on the potential windfall during special events and holidays:

- Raise rates for peak periods.

- Consider implementing a holiday surcharge for specific dates.

Remember to balance profit with guest expectations to avoid turning away potential bookings.

Last-Minute Discounts and Promotions

Last-minute bookings can be a double-edged sword—use them strategically:

- Offer discounts for last-minute bookings to fill unoccupied nights.

- Promote limited-time offers to entice spontaneous travelers.

Balancing Occupancy Rates and Revenue

Finding the sweet spot between high occupancy and optimal revenue is the holy grail of Airbnb pricing:

- **High Occupancy**: Consistent bookings can be a sign of successful pricing, even if rates are lower.

- **High Revenue**: Maximizing revenue often involves strategic rate adjustments.

Striking this balance requires constant monitoring and adjustment based on your goals and market conditions.

The Impact of Cleaning Fees and Additional Charges

Don't forget to factor in cleaning fees and additional charges when setting your rates:

- **Cleaning Fees:** Ensure your cleaning fee covers the cost of cleaning services.

- **Extra Guest Charges:** Charge extra for guests beyond your standard occupancy limit.

Transparently communicate these charges to guests to avoid surprises during the booking process.

Pricing Psychology: The Power of Perception

Pricing isn't just about numbers; it's about how potential guests perceive value:

- **Charm Pricing**: Ending prices with .99 (e.g., $99 instead of $100) can make rates appear more attractive.

- **Discount Psychology**: Highlighting discounts or savings in your listing can capture attention.

Guests often choose properties based on a combination of value, location, and perception of what they're getting for their money.

Consistently Evaluating and Adjusting Your Pricing

Pricing on Airbnb isn't a "set it and forget it" affair. It requires ongoing evaluation and adjustment:

- Regularly review your pricing strategy to ensure it aligns with your goals and market conditions.

- Monitor your competitors and adapt to changes in the market.

- Use guest feedback and reviews to gauge whether your pricing aligns with guest expectations.

Remember, there's no one-size-fits-all approach to pricing on Airbnb. It's a dynamic process that involves balancing various factors to achieve your hosting goals, whether that's maximizing revenue, maintaining high occupancy, or offering competitive rates. The key is to stay flexible, continuously evaluate your strategy, and adapt to the everchanging landscape of Airbnb pricing.

Chapter 7:

Guest Experience: Going Above and Beyond

Welcome to the delightful realm of guest experience, where hospitality isn't just a service; it's an art form that transforms ordinary stays into unforgettable memories. In this chapter, we'll explore the world of creating extraordinary guest experiences that leave your visitors not just satisfied but genuinely delighted.

Creating Memorable Guest Experiences

Let's begin by acknowledging that hosting on Airbnb isn't just about providing a roof and a bed; it's about crafting unique experiences that guests will cherish long after they've checked out.

Understanding the Guest's Journey

To provide exceptional hospitality, it's crucial to step into your guest's shoes and understand their journey:

- **Booking:** The anticipation of their trip begins with the booking process.

- **Pre-Arrival**: Guests plan and prepare for their stay.

- **Arrival**: They arrive at your property with a mix of excitement and curiosity.

- **Stay:** Their actual experience, where comfort, convenience, and enjoyment are paramount.

- **Check-Out**: As they depart, their final impression of their stay is formed.

Every stage of this journey offers opportunities to exceed expectations and create moments that stand out.

Personalization and Attention to Detail

Imagine checking into a hotel, and the staff remembers your name, your favorite drink, and even your preferred pillow type. That's the power of personalization and attention to detail.

- **Welcome Messages:** Send personalized welcome messages to guests before their arrival to make them feel valued.

- **In-Stay Amenities**: Consider special touches like a welcome basket, personalized notes, or treats that align with their preferences.

- **Remembering Special Occasions:** If guests are celebrating a special occasion like a birthday or anniversary, a thoughtful gesture can make their stay unforgettable.

The Importance of Clear and Timely Communication

Effective communication is the backbone of a positive guest experience:

- **Prompt Responses**: Respond to guest inquiries and messages promptly. It shows you're attentive and reliable.

- **Clear Instructions**: Provide clear and concise instructions for check-in, check-out, and any house rules.

- **Local Recommendations:** Share recommendations for local attractions, restaurants, and activities.

Clear and timely communication ensures a smooth and stress-free experience for your guests.

Providing a Warm Welcome

First impressions matter, and a warm welcome sets the tone for the entire stay:

-        **Personal Greeting:** If possible, welcome guests in person with a friendly smile.

-        **Key Handover:** Make the check-in process seamless by providing keys or access instructions.

-        **Orientation:** Offer a brief tour of your property, highlighting key amenities and features.

A warm welcome makes guests feel immediately at ease and valued.

Offering Local Insights and Recommendations

As a host, you're the local expert, and guests often seek your guidance:

-        **Local Insights**: Share insider tips about the area, such as the best coffee shop, hidden gems, or upcoming events.

-        **Customized Recommendations:** Tailor your recommendations to the guest's interests and preferences.

-        **Maps and Guides:** Provide maps and guides to help guests explore your city or region.

Your local knowledge adds a layer of authenticity to their stay.

The Role of Amenities in Guest Satisfaction

Amenities can transform a good stay into a great one:

- **Kitchen Essentials:** Stock your kitchen with essentials like coffee, tea, and basic spices.

- **Entertainment**: Offer entertainment options like books, games, or streaming services.

- **Toiletries:** Provide quality toiletries and ensure there are enough towels and linens.

- **Basic Supplies**: Ensure essential supplies like toilet paper, cleaning products, and trash bags are well-stocked.

A well-prepared space shows you've considered every detail to enhance their comfort.

Quality Bedding and Linens

Nothing says "comfort" like plush bedding and high-quality linens:

- **Comfortable Mattress:** Invest in a comfortable mattress and quality pillows for a good night's sleep.

- **Crisp Linens:** Use clean, high-thread-count sheets that feel luxurious against the skin.

- **Extra Blankets and Pillows**: Provide extra blankets and pillows to accommodate different preferences.

A restful night's sleep can make all the difference in the guest experience.

A Clean and Well-Maintained Property

Cleanliness isn't just a basic expectation; it's a cornerstone of guest satisfaction:

- **Thorough Cleaning:** Ensure your property is spotless before each guest's arrival.

- **Regular Maintenance**: Address any maintenance issues promptly to keep your property in top condition.

- **Attention to Detail:** Pay attention to often-overlooked areas like corners, baseboards, and under furniture.

A clean and well-maintained property speaks volumes about your commitment to guest comfort.

Guest Check-In and Check-Out Processes

Efficient and hassle-free check-in and check-out processes are vital:

- **Detailed Instructions:** Provide clear instructions for both processes, including any access codes or key handovers.

- **Flexibility:** Offer flexibility in check-in and check-out times when possible.

- **Luggage Storage:** Consider providing luggage storage options for guests with early arrivals or late departures.

A smooth process at these junctures can leave a lasting positive impression.

Handling Guest Requests and Special Occasions

Guests may have specific requests or be celebrating special occasions:

-       **Accommodating Requests:** Do your best to fulfill reasonable guest requests, whether it's extra towels or a late checkout.

-       **Celebratory Surprises:** Consider providing a small surprise for guests celebrating birthdays, anniversaries, or other special occasions.

Going the extra mile in these situations can create memorable moments.

Resolving Issues and Concerns Promptly

No stay is without its hiccups. How you handle issues matters:

-       **Open Communication:** Encourage guests to communicate any concerns promptly.

-       **Quick Resolution:** Address issues promptly and professionally, offering solutions and alternatives.

-       **Follow-Up:** After resolving an issue, follow up to ensure the guest is satisfied.

A swift and satisfactory resolution can turn a negative experience into a positive one.

Utilizing Technology for Guest Convenience

Leverage technology to enhance the guest experience:

- **Smart Locks:** Consider using smart locks for keyless entry.

- **Automated Messages:** Use automated messages for check-in instructions, house rules, and local recommendations.

- **Thermostat Control:** If possible, provide a thermostat that guests can adjust for their comfort.

Technology can streamline the guest experience and offer added convenience.

Seeking Guest Feedback and Reviews

Feedback is a valuable tool for improvement:

- **Encourage Reviews:** Encourage guests to leave reviews, sharing their experiences with future travelers.

- **Guest Surveys:** Consider sending post-stay surveys to gather detailed feedback.

- **Feedback Implementation:** Act on constructive feedback to continuously enhance your hosting.

Guest feedback is your compass for improving the guest experience.

Evolving Your Guest Experience Over Time

The world of hospitality is ever-evolving, and so should your guest experience:

- **Stay Updated:** Stay informed about industry trends and evolving guest expectations.

-        **Regular Evaluation:** Continuously assess your guest experience and make adjustments as needed.

-        **Surprise and Delight:** Surprise returning guests with upgrades or special offers to show appreciation.

A dynamic guest experience keeps guests coming back and sharing their positive experiences with others.

In the world of Airbnb hosting, creating memorable guest experiences isn't just about providing accommodation; it's about crafting moments that resonate with your guests long after they've departed. It's about turning ordinary stays into extraordinary memories that guests cherish and share with friends and family.

In this chapter, we've journeyed through the art of hospitality, exploring the various facets that contribute to an exceptional guest experience. From the initial booking stage to the final farewell, each step along the way offers opportunities to exceed expectations and create moments that stand out.

Remember, a memorable guest experience isn't solely about grand gestures or expensive amenities. It's often the small, thoughtful details that leave a lasting impression. Whether it's a personalized welcome message, a local tip, or a surprise treat, these gestures show your guests that you genuinely care about their well-being and enjoyment during their stay.

Furthermore, technology can be a valuable ally in enhancing the guest experience. Smart locks for keyless entry, automated messages for clear instructions, and thermostat controls for comfort are just a few examples of how technology can streamline the guest journey and offer added convenience.

Guest feedback is your compass for improvement. Encourage reviews and guest surveys to gather valuable insights into what you're doing right and where you can make enhancements. Be proactive in seeking feedback and, more importantly, act on constructive suggestions to continuously enhance your hosting.

As a host, it's essential to stay updated on industry trends and evolving guest expectations. The hospitality landscape is dynamic, and what guests seek today may differ from their expectations a year from now. Regularly evaluate your guest experience and make adjustments as needed to stay relevant and competitive.

Finally, consider surprise-and-delight tactics for returning guests. Show your appreciation by offering upgrades, discounts, or special offers. These small gestures can go a long way in building guest loyalty and encouraging repeat bookings.

In the world of Airbnb hosting, creating extraordinary guest experiences is both an art and a science. It's about going above and beyond to make your guests feel welcomed, valued, and pampered. By embracing the principles and strategies outlined in this chapter, you'll not only elevate your hosting game but also leave a trail of delighted guests who can't wait to return to your slice of hospitality heaven. So, go ahead, craft those magical moments, and make every stay an unforgettable adventure!

Chapter 8:

Guest Communication: Building Positive Relationships

Ah, the art of communication! In the realm of Airbnb hosting, effective communication is not just a skill; it's the cornerstone of building positive relationships with your guests. In this chapter, we'll embark on a journey through the wonderful world of guest communication, exploring how to nurture connections, set clear expectations, and create a hospitality experience that leaves a lasting impression.

Effective Pre-Booking Communication

It all begins before the booking is even made. Your prebooking communication sets the tone for the entire guest experience. Here's how to get it right:

Responding Promptly to Inquiry Messages

When a potential guest sends you an inquiry or message, be swift in your response. Timeliness shows that you're attentive and reliable.

The Importance of Professionalism

While it's vital to be friendly and approachable, maintaining professionalism in your communication is equally crucial. This means using polite language, addressing guests respectfully, and refraining from inappropriate or overly casual language.

Setting Clear Expectations

One of the most valuable things you can do as a host is to set clear expectations right from the start. Don't leave anything to chance:

-        **House Rules:** Communicate your house rules clearly so that guests know what's expected of them.

-        **Amenities:** Describe the amenities available and any limitations, so guests aren't surprised.

-        **Check-In/Check-Out Times:** Specify your check-in and check-out times to avoid misunderstandings.

By doing so, you minimize the risk of miscommunication and ensure a smooth guest experience.

Addressing Questions and Concerns

Be open to questions and concerns from potential guests. Respond with patience and provide detailed information to address their queries. A helpful and informative response can go a long way in winning a booking.

Welcoming First-Time Airbnb Guests

For guests who are new to Airbnb, your role as a host is even more critical. They may have uncertainties and require extra guidance. Be prepared to walk them through the booking process, explain how your property works, and offer reassurance about the safety and reliability of Airbnb.

Nurturing Repeat Business and Loyalty

Building lasting relationships with guests is a rewarding aspect of hosting. Treat your returning guests like old friends:

Recognition: Acknowledge returning guests and express your appreciation for their loyalty.

- **Special Offers:** Consider offering discounts or perks for repeat bookings.

- **Personalization:** Remember details about their previous stays, such as their favorite room or preferences.

These gestures make guests feel valued and encourage them to choose your property for future trips.

Communication Dos and Don'ts

As you navigate the world of guest communication, here are some important dos and don'ts to keep in mind:

- **Do:** Be responsive, polite, and professional in all your communications.

- **Don't:** Use offensive or inappropriate language, or engage in confrontational discussions.

Remember, your communication style reflects on your hospitality and influences the overall guest experience.

Handling Booking Confirmations and Reservations

Once a guest has booked your property, send a warm and appreciative confirmation message. Express your excitement about their upcoming stay and provide any additional information they might need, such as payment details or house rules.

Proactive Communication Prior to Check-In

Leading up to the guest's arrival, send proactive messages to ensure they have everything they need:

Directions: Provide clear directions to your property, including any special instructions for parking or access.

- **Check-In Information:** Detail the check-in process, including any codes or keys they'll need.

- **Contact Information:** Share your contact information in case they need to reach you before or during their stay.

Providing Directions and Arrival Information

Guests appreciate clear and concise information about how to get to your property:

Maps and Directions: Include maps and step-by-step directions, especially if your property is in a remote or tricky-to-find location.

- **Local Tips:** Share local insights, such as the best nearby restaurants or attractions.

Making their journey to your property as smooth as possible is a great way to start their stay on a positive note.

Welcoming Guests Upon Arrival

If possible, welcome guests in person with a friendly smile and a warm greeting. If an in-person welcome isn't feasible, consider leaving a personalized note or a welcome basket to make them feel immediately at home.

Communicating During the Guest's Stay

Maintaining communication during a guest's stay is essential for addressing any questions, concerns, or needs that may arise:

Accessibility: Be readily available for any questions or issues they might have.

- **Local Assistance:** Offer help with restaurant reservations, transportation, or anything else that can enhance their stay.

- **Check-In**: Check in with guests periodically to ensure they're comfortable and satisfied.

Being Available for Emergencies

Emergencies can happen, and guests need to know they can rely on you:

- **Emergency Contacts:** Provide emergency contact information, including local authorities and medical facilities.

- **Quick Response:** Respond promptly to urgent messages and take action to assist as needed.

Guests should feel safe and supported throughout their stay, even in challenging situations.

Post-Stay Follow-Up and Feedback Requests

After guests check out, send a thank-you message expressing your gratitude for choosing your property.

Invite them to leave a review and provide feedback about their stay.

Guest feedback is invaluable for improvement, and it's also a way to keep the lines of communication open for future bookings.

In the world of Airbnb hosting, building positive relationships through effective communication is not just a strategy; it's a philosophy. By mastering the art of thoughtful, timely, and respectful communication, you create an environment where guests feel valued, respected, and cared for. These connections, built on trust and hospitality, are what transform a one-time booking into a lifelong friendship. So, keep those messages friendly, those responses prompt, and those conversations engaging. As you navigate the intricate world of guest communication, remember that it's not just about conveying information; it's about fostering connections, setting expectations, and creating an environment where every guest feels like an honored friend.

Effective pre-booking communication is your first opportunity to make a positive impression on potential guests. Responding promptly to inquiries, maintaining professionalism, and setting clear expectations are the foundational elements of this phase. Think of this as the opening act of a great story, where you captivate your audience and set the stage for a memorable experience.

Addressing questions and concerns with patience and informative responses can turn a hesitant guest into a confident one. For first-time Airbnb users, your guidance can be a beacon of reassurance, helping them navigate the booking process with ease.

As you host returning guests, you embark on a delightful journey of building guest loyalty and repeat business. Recognizing and appreciating their loyalty, offering special incentives, and personalizing their experience are the keys to ensuring they return to your hospitality haven time and time again.

Throughout your communication journey, it's crucial to adhere to dos and don'ts that reflect the professionalism and respect that guests deserve. Being responsive, polite, and professional in your communication is a universal rule. On the flip side, avoiding offensive or inappropriate language and steering clear of confrontational discussions is equally important. Your communication style reflects not only on you as a host but also on the overall guest experience.

Once a guest has made a booking, your booking confirmation and reservation messages should exude warmth and appreciation. Express your excitement about their upcoming stay and provide any necessary details to ensure a seamless experience.

In the lead-up to check-in, proactive communication takes the spotlight. Share directions, check-in information, and local tips to ease the guest's journey to your property. This proactive approach minimizes any anxiety or confusion guests might experience as they make their way to your delightful abode.

When the moment arrives for your guests to step foot into their temporary home, a warm and personal welcome can make all the difference. If you can greet them in person, it's a fantastic way to establish a connection. If not, consider leaving a handwritten note or a welcome basket to convey your warm regards.

Throughout their stay, maintaining open lines of communication is essential. Be accessible for questions or assistance, and offer your insights and recommendations to enhance their experience. Regular check-ins with guests can ensure their comfort and satisfaction, making them feel valued and cared for.

Of course, emergencies can happen, and guests need to know they can rely on you in such situations. Provide emergency contact information and respond promptly to urgent messages, taking the necessary steps to assist guests in distress.

As guests prepare to check out and bid farewell to your hospitality haven, a post-stay thank-you message is a gracious way to express your gratitude for choosing your property. Invite them to leave a review and provide feedback about their stay. Guest feedback is not only valuable for improvement but also for maintaining a connection with guests for future bookings.

In the realm of Airbnb hosting, communication is the glue that binds the entire guest experience together. It's the thread that weaves a narrative of warmth, trust, and care throughout their journey. So, keep those lines of communication open, those messages friendly, and those conversations engaging. In doing so, you'll not only create wonderful memories for your guests but also lay the foundation for a thriving hosting venture filled with positive relationships and returning friends.

Chapter 9:

Handling Difficult Situations with Grace

Ah, the rollercoaster ride of hosting on Airbnb! While the majority of your hosting journey will be filled with delightful guests and memorable experiences, there may come a time when you encounter a few bumps in the road. In this chapter, we'll equip you with the skills and strategies to handle these challenging situations with grace, finesse, and a touch of humor.

Preparing for Common Challenges

Every host's journey is unique, but there are some challenges that commonly crop up in the world of hospitality. By preparing for these potential hurdles in advance, you can navigate them more effectively when they arise.

Dealing with Guest Complaints

Guest complaints can range from minor inconveniences to more significant issues. The key is to listen attentively, empathize with their concerns, and take prompt action to address the problem. Remember, a complaint is an opportunity to turn a negative experience into a positive one.

Managing Booking Cancellations

Cancellations can be disappointing for both hosts and guests. Understanding Airbnb's cancellation policies and having a clear, empathetic communication strategy can help you manage these situations while minimizing negative impacts.

Addressing Property Damage and Accidents

Accidents happen, and sometimes they result in property damage. Having a plan in place for addressing and resolving such incidents can save you time and stress. It's also wise to consider whether security deposits or insurance can help protect your property.

Navigating Guest Disputes and Conflicts

If disputes or conflicts arise between guests sharing your space, your role as a mediator becomes crucial. Diplomacy, active listening, and clear communication are your allies in resolving these situations peacefully.

Resolving Issues Amicably

Aim for amicable resolutions in all situations. This not only ensures guest satisfaction but also helps maintain your hosting reputation. Find common ground, propose solutions, and work collaboratively to reach an agreement.

Enforcing House Rules and Policies

Your house rules and policies are there for a reason. Be firm but fair in enforcing them. Communicate rules clearly from the start, and address any violations promptly and professionally.

Handling Difficult Guests with Diplomacy

Sometimes, you may encounter guests who are challenging to host. Patience, diplomacy, and professionalism are your best tools for managing difficult personalities and ensuring a positive experience for other guests.

Dealing with Noise and Disturbance Complaints

Noise complaints are among the most common issues hosts face. Address them promptly, and if necessary, consider implementing quiet hours and providing clear guidance on noise expectations.

Emergency Procedures and Contacts

Prepare for emergencies by having a clear set of procedures and contact information readily available. Ensure guests know what to do in case of fire, medical emergencies, or other unexpected situations.

Working with Airbnb Support

Airbnb offers support to hosts when needed. Familiarize yourself with their support system, including how to contact Airbnb for assistance with reservations, disputes, or other issues.

Documenting Incidents and Communications

Keep detailed records of incidents, complaints, and communications with guests. This documentation can be invaluable in case disputes escalate or require Airbnb's intervention.

Insurance and Liability Considerations

Review your insurance coverage and liability considerations as a host. Understand what is and isn't covered, and consider additional coverage options to protect your property and finances.

Learning from Challenging Situations

Challenging situations can be valuable learning experiences. After each incident, take the time to reflect on what went well and what could have been handled differently. Use these insights to continuously improve your hosting skills.

Continuously Improving Your Hosting Skills

Your journey as a host is a continuous evolution. Embrace the challenges as opportunities for growth, refine your hosting strategies, and commit to providing exceptional experiences for your guests.

Remember, hosting on Airbnb is an adventure filled with delightful surprises and the occasional hiccup. With the right mindset, preparation, and a dash of grace, you can navigate these challenges like a seasoned pro, ensuring that your hosting journey remains a rewarding and enjoyable one. So, let's dive into the art of handling difficult situations with style and grace!

Chapter 10:

Cleaning and Maintenance: Keeping Your Property Pristine

Welcome to the backstage of Airbnb hosting, where the magic truly happens—maintaining a clean and well-kept property. In this chapter, we'll explore the art of ensuring your place shines brighter than a supernova, impressing guests, and keeping them coming back for more. Get ready to dive into the world of cleaning and maintenance with style and expertise!

The Importance of a Clean and Well-Maintained Property

Let's start with the basics: a spotless and well-maintained property is the foundation of a positive guest experience. Think of it as the canvas upon which you paint the masterpiece of hospitality. A clean and well-kept space not only wows guests but also helps maintain the longevity of your property.

Setting Cleaning Standards and Checklists

Consistency is the name of the game when it comes to cleaning. Develop detailed cleaning standards and checklists that leave no nook or cranny unattended. This ensures that every clean is up to par, regardless of who's doing the cleaning.

Scheduling and Managing Cleanings Efficiently

Time is of the essence in the world of Airbnb. Efficient scheduling and management of cleanings are crucial for rapid turnovers between bookings. Create a well-organized system to handle the cleaning process seamlessly.

Ensuring Quality and Consistency

Quality control is your secret weapon. Regularly inspect your property to ensure that it meets your high standards of cleanliness and maintenance. Consistency in this regard is key to earning top-notch reviews.

Proper Disposal of Waste and Recycling

Do your part for the environment by educating yourself on local waste and recycling regulations. Provide clear instructions to guests on how to dispose of waste properly, including recycling, composting, and trash.

Deep Cleaning and Seasonal Maintenance

Besides regular cleaning, consider deep cleaning sessions to keep your property in top shape. Seasonal maintenance, such as HVAC system checks or gutter cleanings, ensures that your property is ready for whatever weather Mother Nature throws its way.

Handling Repairs and Property Upkeep

Property maintenance isn't just about cleanliness; it's also about functionality. Promptly address repairs and upkeep tasks to keep everything in tip-top condition. A smoothly running property is a happy property.

Securing Your Property and Guests' Belongings

Safety is paramount in hospitality. Secure your property to protect both your assets and your guests' belongings.

Install safety features like smoke detectors, locks, and security cameras as needed.

Pest Control and Prevention Strategies

Nobody likes uninvited guests of the creepy-crawly variety. Implement pest control and prevention strategies to ensure that your property remains a pest-free paradise. Regular inspections and sealing entry points can work wonders.

Preparing for Guest Arrivals

Guests expect a pristine space upon arrival, so make sure your property is impeccably clean and well-stocked with essentials. A warm and welcoming environment sets the stage for a delightful stay.

Rapid Turnaround Between Bookings

Airbnb hosts are known for their quick turnovers between bookings. This means efficient cleaning, restocking, and ensuring that everything is in perfect working order. Time management is your ally here.

Partnering with Cleaning and Maintenance Services

If you're not a cleaning pro yourself, consider partnering with cleaning and maintenance services. They can take the reins and ensure your property stays in pristine condition. Just be sure to communicate your standards clearly.

Managing Cleaning Costs

Budgeting for cleaning and maintenance is part of the hosting game. Strike a balance between quality and cost efficiency. Remember that cleanliness is an investment that pays off in positive reviews and repeat bookings.

Guest Check-Out Inspections

Inspect the property after each guest check-out to identify any damage or missing items. Address issues promptly and, if necessary, communicate with guests about any concerns. Document these inspections for your records.

Maintaining a Safe and Welcoming Environment

Ultimately, your goal is to maintain a safe and welcoming environment for your guests. This includes addressing any safety hazards, providing clear instructions, and creating a space where guests feel at home.

In the world of Airbnb hosting, cleaning and maintenance are the unsung heroes that make the show go on. With meticulous attention to detail, a well-organized approach, and a commitment to cleanliness, you'll not only dazzle guests but also ensure the longevity of your hosting venture. So, roll up those sleeves, equip yourself with the finest cleaning supplies, and let's make your property shine brighter than a supernova!

Chapter 11:

Legalities and Regulations: Navigating the Airbnb Landscape

Ah, the world of Airbnb hosting, where the path to hospitality stardom is paved with sparkling reviews and cozy bed linens. But amidst the excitement, it's vital to keep your legal ducks in a row. In this chapter, we'll demystify the labyrinth of legalities and regulations that come with hosting on Airbnb, all while maintaining our sense of humor.

Understanding Local Laws and Regulations

Before you dive headfirst into hosting, take a step back and understand the local laws and regulations that govern short-term rentals in your area. These can vary widely, from city to city and even neighborhood to neighborhood. What's allowed in one place might be strictly prohibited a few blocks away.

Zoning and Land Use Regulations

Zoning regulations are the silent architects of your hosting adventure. They determine whether your property can be used for short-term rentals, long-term rentals, or if it's strictly residential. Check your local zoning codes to ensure you're on the right side of the law.

Licensing and Permits for Short-Term Rentals

Some places require hosts to obtain licenses or permits to legally rent their properties on a short-term basis. Be sure to research whether your locale has such requirements and, if so, follow the necessary procedures.

Taxation and Reporting Requirements

Taxation isn't just a buzzkill; it's a legal obligation. Different jurisdictions have various tax rules for short-term rentals. Ensure you understand your responsibilities regarding occupancy taxes, sales taxes, and income reporting.

Compliance with Building Codes and Safety Standards

Safety first! Your property should meet all applicable building codes and safety standards. This includes essentials like smoke detectors, fire extinguishers, and proper exits. Not only is it the law, but it's also common sense.

Health and Sanitation Regulations

Cleanliness isn't just about impressing guests; it's a legal requirement. Follow health and sanitation regulations to the letter. Regular deep cleaning and proper waste disposal are your allies in this endeavor.

Insurance Considerations for Hosts

Insurance is your safety net in the unpredictable world of hosting. Consult your insurance provider to ensure your policy covers short-term rentals. A small investment now can save you from significant headaches later.

Liability and Guest Injury Concerns

Guests are like family, but sometimes accidents happen. Protect yourself by understanding liability laws and ensuring your property is safe. Document any safety features and include clear instructions in your guest guide.

Contracts and Rental Agreements

A good old-fashioned contract can work wonders in preventing misunderstandings. Create a solid rental agreement that outlines house rules, cancellation policies, and any other important terms. Both you and your guests should sign it.

Handling Security Deposits

Security deposits are like a financial safety blanket. Clearly define the terms for holding and returning deposits in your rental agreement. Use them wisely to cover damages or unpaid fees.

Data Privacy and Guest Information

Respecting guest privacy is paramount. Ensure you handle guest data, such as names and contact information, responsibly and in compliance with data protection laws.

Dispute Resolution Mechanisms

Even the happiest homes can have hiccups. Establish a dispute resolution mechanism to handle guest grievances. Airbnb offers a resolution center, but you can also include your process in your rental agreement.

Navigating Lease Agreements and Landlord Permissions

If you're renting the property you're hosting on Airbnb, be aware of your lease agreement's terms and your landlord's permissions. Violating your lease could lead to eviction.

Keeping Up with Evolving Regulations

The only constant in the hosting world is change. Keep your finger on the pulse of evolving regulations and adapt accordingly. Follow local news, join host communities, and stay informed.

Legal Resources and Professional Advice

When in doubt, seek professional advice. Lawyers, accountants, and real estate professionals can provide invaluable guidance to ensure you're on the right side of the law.

Remember, being a responsible host isn't just about providing a comfy bed and fluffy towels; it's about being a good citizen and respecting the legal framework of your community. By mastering the legalities and regulations of Airbnb hosting, you can rest easy, knowing you're not just a gracious host, but also a law-abiding one. So, let's embark on this legal journey with a smile, a notepad, and a penchant for compliance!

Chapter 12:

Expanding Your Airbnb Portfolio

So, you've caught the Airbnb bug, and your hosting adventure is in full swing. But wait, there's more! In this chapter, we're diving into the exhilarating world of expanding your Airbnb portfolio. We'll explore everything from assessing your readiness to becoming a multi-property maestro—all with a sprinkle of humor and a dash of insider knowledge.

Assessing Your Readiness to Expand

First things first, are you ready to level up your hosting game? Expanding your Airbnb portfolio isn't just about more listings; it's a commitment to scaling your operation. Assess your time, resources, and determination to embark on this journey.

Identifying Market Opportunities

Before you dive into expanding, let's talk strategy. Identify market opportunities that align with your goals. Analyze demand, competition, and emerging trends. Knowing where to expand is half the battle.

Scaling Up Your Hosting Operation

Scaling up means stepping up your hosting game. Are you ready to take on more responsibilities, from cleaning to guest communications? Consider your bandwidth and whether you need to enlist help.

Financing Your Airbnb Investments

Money talks, especially in real estate. Explore your financing options, from traditional mortgages to Airbnb specific loans. Calculate the costs, down payments, and interest rates to determine what suits your budget.

Analyzing Investment Risks and Rewards

Investing in real estate comes with its share of risks and rewards. Carefully analyze both sides of the coin. Consider factors like property appreciation, rental income, and potential market fluctuations.

Property Selection and Location Strategies

Choosing the right properties is the name of the game. Research neighborhoods, assess property conditions, and think about your target audience. Location isn't just about proximity to attractions; it's also about safety and appeal.

Evaluating Potential Returns on Investment

Let's get down to the numbers. Calculate potential returns on your investments. Factor in expenses like mortgage payments, property management fees, and maintenance costs. Positive cash flow is the goal.

The Role of Property Management Companies

Scaling up might mean needing extra hands on deck. Property management companies can handle tasks like cleaning, guest communication, and maintenance. Find the right partner to lighten your load.

Developing a Diversified Portfolio

Diversification is the spice of Airbnb life. Consider different property types and locations. Diversifying can help you weather market fluctuations and attract a broader range of guests.

Financing Options for Property Acquisition

There's more than one way to finance your property acquisitions. From traditional loans to peer-to-peer lending, explore the financing options that align with your goals and financial situation.

Building Partnerships and Networks

Success often comes from who you know. Build partnerships with local businesses, property managers, and other hosts. Networking can open doors to opportunities and support.

Legal and Tax Considerations for Multiple Properties

With great hosting comes great responsibility—especially in the eyes of the law and the taxman. Consult legal and tax professionals to ensure you're compliant and optimized for tax benefits.

The Art of Property Staging and Design

Aesthetic appeal matters. Invest in property staging and design to make your listings stand out. Think comfy beds, stylish decor, and Instagram-worthy corners.

Marketing Strategies for Multiple Listings

More listings mean more marketing. Develop a strategy to showcase your portfolio effectively. Professional photos, well-crafted descriptions, and strategic pricing are your allies.

Managing Multiple Properties Efficiently

Efficiency is your superpower when managing multiple properties. Use technology to streamline tasks, and establish processes that keep everything running smoothly.

Expanding your Airbnb portfolio is like leveling up in a video game; it's challenging but oh-so-rewarding. Whether you're a one-property wonder or a multi-listing maestro, this journey can lead to financial freedom and a deeper connection to the world of hospitality. So, put on your expansion cap, grab your toolkit, and let's build your empire—one guest at a time!

Chapter 13:

Airbnb Investment Strategies: Buying and Managing Properties

Welcome to the big leagues of Airbnb hosting – property ownership! In this chapter, we'll delve deep into the world of Airbnb investment strategies. From assessing your financial readiness to growing your real estate portfolio, we've got all the secrets to help you become a property magnate while keeping your sense of humor intact.

Assessing Your Financial Readiness

Before you jump into the wonderful world of property ownership, take a good, hard look at your finances. Do you have the funds for a down payment, renovation, and ongoing expenses? Property ownership is like a long-term relationship; it takes commitment.

Understanding Your Investment Goals

Why do you want to invest in Airbnb properties? Is it for steady rental income, property appreciation, or something else entirely? Understanding your investment goals is the first step to crafting a successful strategy.

The Pros and Cons of Property Ownership

Property ownership isn't all rainbows and sunshine. It comes with pros like building equity and cons like property management responsibilities. We'll explore both sides so you know what you're getting into.

Financing Your Airbnb Property

How are you going to finance your dream Airbnb property? Will it be through a traditional mortgage, Airbnb-specific loan, or other creative financing options? Let's crunch the numbers and see what fits your budget.

Property Selection and Location Criteria

Location, location, location! We can't stress this enough. The right location can make or break your Airbnb property. We'll dive into the criteria for selecting the perfect spot that suits your investment goals.

Evaluating Potential Properties

So many properties, so little time! We'll discuss how to evaluate potential properties based on your investment goals, budget, and location criteria. It's like a real estate treasure hunt!

Due Diligence in Property Acquisition

Don't let your excitement overshadow due diligence. We'll guide you through the essential checks, inspections, and legal processes involved in acquiring a property.

Renovation and Upgrading for Airbnb

Sometimes, properties need a little TLC to shine on Airbnb. Learn the ins and outs of renovating and upgrading your property to make it guest-ready and Instagram-worthy.

Property Management Options

Managing properties can be a full-time gig. We'll explore your options, from DIY property management to hiring professionals or property management companies. Choose the one that suits your lifestyle.

Short-Term vs. Long-Term Rentals

Is short-term or long-term rental your jam? We'll compare the two, weighing the pros and cons of each to help you decide which aligns with your investment goals.

Co-Living and Group Accommodations

Explore the exciting world of co-living and group accommodations. This niche can be a lucrative option if you're interested in catering to larger groups or longer stays.

Specialty Niche Markets

Speaking of niches, there are specialized markets waiting to be explored. From pet-friendly rentals to themed accommodations, we'll unlock the potential of niche markets.

Creating an Attractive Property Listing

The listing is your property's virtual storefront. We'll share tips and tricks to create listings that draw in guests and make your property irresistible.

Property Ownership and Tax Implications

With great property ownership comes great tax responsibility. We'll cover the tax implications, deductions, and benefits of being a property owner.

Growing Your Real Estate Portfolio Over Time

Once you've got a taste of property ownership, you might want to expand your real estate empire. We'll discuss strategies for growing your portfolio over time and achieving your investment dreams.

Property ownership isn't just about owning a piece of real estate; it's about becoming a savvy investor and hospitality pro. With the right strategy and a dose of ambition, you can turn your Airbnb investments into a lucrative, long-term endeavor. So, grab your financial calculator and let's embark on this exciting journey into the world of Airbnb property ownership!

Chapter 14:

Automating Your Airbnb Business for Passive Income

Welcome to the future of Airbnb hosting, where technology and automation combine forces to make your hosting dreams come true. In this chapter, we'll uncover the secrets of automating your Airbnb business, turning it into a well-oiled machine that generates passive income while you sip cocktails on a beach. Well, maybe not quite, but close enough!

The Importance of Automation

Let's kick things off by acknowledging the elephant in the room: automation is a game-changer. It frees up your time, reduces stress, and allows you to focus on the parts of hosting you truly enjoy. It's like having a personal assistant who never complains.

Identifying Repetitive Tasks and Processes

To automate effectively, you need to identify those repetitive tasks and processes that eat up your time. Think guest communications, calendar management, and cleaning schedules. Identifying them is like finding the low hanging fruit of efficiency.

Utilizing Technology for Efficiency

Thank goodness for technology! There's an app or software for almost every aspect of hosting. We'll explore tools that help you automate your business, from guest messaging platforms to property management systems.

Managing Reservations and Calendar Updates

Keeping your calendar up-to-date can be a hassle. Automate reservation management and calendar updates to prevent double bookings and ensure a smooth hosting experience.

Automated Guest Communication

Forget about sending welcome messages manually. Automate guest communication with pre-set messages for booking confirmations, check-in instructions, and post stay follow-ups. It's like having a virtual concierge.

Keyless Entry and Smart Locks

Say goodbye to physical keys. Invest in smart locks for keyless entry, allowing guests to check in with a unique code or smartphone app. It's not only convenient but also enhances security.

Housekeeping and Cleaning Services

Managing housekeeping can be a chore. Consider outsourcing to cleaning services that follow automated schedules and checklists. Your property will sparkle like a diamond without you lifting a finger.

Pricing and Rate Optimization Tools

Pricing can make or break your income. Use pricing tools that analyze demand, competition, and local events to optimize your rates automatically. It's like having a revenue manager on call.

Guest Check-In and Check-Out Automation

Automate guest check-in with digital access codes and self-check-in instructions. When guests depart, automate the check-out process, making room for your next happy visitors.

Property Surveillance and Security

Keep an eye on your property with automated surveillance systems. From security cameras to smart sensors, technology adds an extra layer of protection.

Maintenance and Repair Automation

Regular maintenance is key to keeping your property in top shape. Schedule automated maintenance reminders and work orders for repairs. No more sticky faucets or flickering lights.

Outsourcing Administrative Tasks

Running a remote empire? Consider outsourcing administrative tasks to virtual assistants. They can handle everything from guest communications to calendar management, leaving you with more time for strategic decisions.

Monitoring and Analytics for Performance

Use monitoring and analytics tools to track your property's performance. From occupancy rates to guest reviews, data driven insights help you make informed decisions.

Building a Remote Hosting Team

As you expand, consider building a remote hosting team. Delegate tasks to property managers, cleaners, and guest relations experts. It's the ultimate step toward true passive income.

Achieving Passive Income and Freedom

The ultimate goal of automation is achieving passive income and the freedom to enjoy it. While it may not involve sipping cocktails on a beach 24/7, it means less stress, more efficiency, and the ability to focus on the things that matter most to you.

Automation is your ticket to hosting success with minimal stress. By embracing technology and streamlining your processes, you can turn your Airbnb business into a well-oiled machine that generates income while you get to enjoy the true perks of hosting. So, why wait? Let's automate your way to passive income and freedom – one smart lock and automated message at a time!

Chapter 15:

Collaborating with Airbnb Co-Hosts and Management Services

Congratulations! You've reached the pinnacle of Airbnb hosting where you're not just managing properties; you're orchestrating a symphony of hospitality. In this chapter, we're going to dive deep into the world of collaborating with Airbnb co-hosts and property management services. It's like forming your Avengers team but for hosting!

Understanding Co-Hosting in Airbnb

First, let's demystify co-hosting. Co-hosting involves partnering with individuals or companies to manage your Airbnb listings. Think of it as sharing the hosting load and expertise.

The Benefits of Co-Hosting

Why should you consider co-hosting? Well, there's strength in numbers! Co-hosts bring their skills, time, and local knowledge to the table. They can help you provide a topnotch guest experience.

Finding and Selecting Co-Hosts

Choosing the right co-host is crucial. Look for people or organizations with a track record of successful hosting, stellar communication skills, and a passion for the job.

Establishing Clear Roles and Responsibilities

To avoid any confusion or conflicts, establish clear roles and responsibilities. Who handles guest check-ins? Who manages the cleaning crew? Define it all so your co-hosting ship sails smoothly.

Collaborative Strategies for Success

Collaboration is the name of the game. Work with your cohosts to create strategies for everything from pricing and guest communications to property maintenance and reviews management.

Coordinating Communication with Co-Hosts

Communication is key. Use digital tools and platforms to coordinate with your co-hosts efficiently. It's like having a virtual HQ for your hosting operation.

Handling Guest Inquiries and Bookings

Who handles guest inquiries and bookings? Ensure a seamless process for managing inquiries, accepting bookings, and handling pre-stay communication.

Sharing Revenue and Profit Margins

Money talks, right? Decide on a fair revenue-sharing model with your co-hosts. Whether it's a percentage of the earnings or a fixed fee, make sure everyone's on the same page.

The Role of Property Management Services

Property management services can be a game-changer. They take care of everything from cleaning to maintenance.

It's like having an entire hospitality crew at your disposal.

Identifying Reputable Management Companies

Not all property management companies are created equal. Do your due diligence to find reputable ones that align with your hosting goals and values.

Evaluating Management Agreements

Before you sign on the dotted line, carefully review management agreements. Ensure they cover all aspects of property management, including fees, responsibilities, and terms.

Cost vs. Convenience in Property Management

Consider the trade-off between cost and convenience. While property management services come at a price, they can free up your time and reduce stress significantly.

Leveraging the Expertise of Professionals

Property management professionals know the ins and outs of the industry. Leverage their expertise to enhance guest experiences and maximize your profits.

Maintaining Oversight and Quality Control

Even with co-hosts or property management services, maintain oversight. Regularly review performance, guest feedback, and property conditions to ensure quality control.

Scaling Your Hosting Business with Co-Hosts and Management Services

As you grow, consider scaling your hosting business by adding more co-hosts or properties under management services. Think of it as building your Airbnb empire, one cohost at a time.

Collaborating with co-hosts and property management services is your passport to scaling your hosting business while maintaining quality and sanity. It's about working smarter, not harder. So, gather your co-hosting Avengers, enlist the help of property management heroes, and let's conquer the world of Airbnb together!

Chapter 16:

Accounting and Taxation: Managing Your Airbnb Finances

Ah, the sweet smell of success! You've mastered the art of hosting, but now it's time to tackle a less glamorous but equally important aspect of your Airbnb journey: managing your finances and taxes. Don't worry; we'll make accounting and taxation as engaging as a gripping thriller!

The Financial Side of Airbnb Hosting

Let's face it; Airbnb hosting isn't just about meeting new people and earning rave reviews. It's also about managing the cold, hard cash that flows in and out of your hosting venture. So, grab your calculator; it's time to get financially savvy!

Tracking Income and Expenses

Start by tracking every dime that enters and exits your hosting universe. Income from bookings, cleaning fees, and those occasional late-night snack runs—all of it needs to be accounted for.

Record-Keeping and Documentation

In the world of taxes, documentation is your shield and sword. Maintain meticulous records of every transaction, reservation, and expense. Digital or paper, choose your accounting armor wisely.

The Importance of Separate Banking

Avoid the dreaded mixing of personal and Airbnb funds. Set up a separate bank account for your hosting earnings and expenses. It's like building a financial fortress around your personal savings.

Tax Implications for Airbnb Hosts

The taxman cometh! Understand the tax implications of being an Airbnb host. It varies by location, so familiarize yourself with the local tax laws that affect you.

Understanding Deductions and Write-Offs

Good news! Hosting expenses are your secret weapon against high taxes. Dive into the world of deductions and write-offs for items like cleaning supplies, linens, and even a portion of your rent or mortgage.

Working with Accountants and Tax Advisors

When taxes start feeling like a foreign language, enlist the help of financial experts. Accountants and tax advisors can decipher the code, ensuring you're not paying a cent more than you should.

Legal Structures for Airbnb Businesses

Explore the legal structures for your Airbnb business. Sole proprietorship, LLC, or corporation? Each has its own tax implications and liability protections. Choose wisely, young Padawan.

Quarterly and Annual Tax Obligations

Prepare for a dance with the tax calendar. Some jurisdictions require quarterly payments, while others settle for an annual rendezvous. Keep those dates in your financial rolodex.

Navigating Tax Changes and Updates

Tax laws are about as stable as a Jenga tower in an earthquake. Stay informed about changes and updates in tax regulations that might affect your hosting income.

Compliance with Local Tax Laws

Don't let unpaid taxes become the Airbnb ghost that haunts your dreams. Ensure full compliance with local tax laws, including occupancy taxes, tourist taxes, and the like.

Managing Cash Flow and Reserves

A wise host knows that cash flow is king. Manage your hosting income wisely, setting aside reserves for property maintenance, unexpected expenses, and, of course, taxes.

Budgeting for Property Maintenance

Speaking of property maintenance, budget for it like a pro. From regular upkeep to occasional renovations, it's all part of the game.

Financial Tools and Software for Hosts

Embrace the digital age with financial tools and software designed for hosts. They can automate expense tracking, generate tax reports, and make your life easier.

Building Wealth and Savings through Airbnb

Remember, your Airbnb venture isn't just about paying the bills; it's a pathway to building wealth. Invest your earnings wisely, consider real estate opportunities, and watch your wealth grow.

Managing your Airbnb finances and taxes might not be the most thrilling aspect of hosting, but it's essential for your long-term success. So, roll up your sleeves, get cozy with your spreadsheets, and turn your financial journey into a blockbuster success story. Who knows, maybe one day you'll be hosting financial planning workshops for fellow hosts!

Chapter 17:

Capitalizing on Airbnb Trends and Seasonal Peaks

Welcome to the rollercoaster world of Airbnb, where the only constant is change. In this chapter, we're going to explore how to ride the waves of Airbnb trends and seasonal peaks, turning them into exhilarating opportunities for hosting success.

Embracing the Dynamic Nature of Airbnb

First things first, understand that Airbnb is like a chameleon; it adapts to ever-changing trends and seasons. As a host, you're in the business of adaptability.

Identifying Seasonal Trends and Peaks

Your Airbnb journey is marked by seasons. Identify when your location experiences peaks in tourism and capitalize on them. It's like being the conductor of your own hosting

Preparing Your Property for High Seasons

High seasons call for high preparation. Get your property in tip-top shape before the rush hits. It's like a pre-show backstage makeover for your listing.

Setting Competitive Rates During Peaks

Pricing is your magic wand during peak seasons. Study the competition, adjust your rates accordingly, and watch the bookings flood in. It's like a bidding war, but you're the auctioneer.

Marketing Strategies for Seasonal Demand

When the demand is high, your marketing game should be higher. Utilize eye-catching promotions, social media, and Airbnb's own promotional tools to attract guests. Think of it as your hosting encore.

Capitalizing on Special Events and Holidays

Special events and holidays are golden opportunities. Tailor your listing to these occasions, whether it's decorating for Halloween or offering a romantic Valentine's Day package. Be the host with a theme!

Customizing Your Property for Themes

Get creative with property customization. If it's Christmas, add twinkling lights and a festive tree. If it's a music festival season, offer instruments for impromptu jam sessions. It's like creating a new world for your guests.

Managing High-Volume Bookings

High season often means high volume. Be prepared for quick turnovers, efficient cleanings, and seamless check-ins. You're the ringmaster of a bustling circus, and the show must go on!

Hosting during Off-Peak Seasons

Don't despair during off-peak seasons. Embrace them as opportunities for rest, renovation, and local exploration. It's like taking a deep breath before the next big wave.

Maximizing Earnings Throughout the Year

Your hosting business shouldn't be a one-hit-wonder. Aim for consistent earnings by making the most of both peak and off-peak times.

Monitoring Local Events and Attractions

Keep your finger on the pulse of your local area. Be aware of upcoming events, attractions, and developments that might affect your property's appeal.

Keeping Your Property Fresh and Appealing

Your property is your canvas; keep it fresh and appealing. Regularly update decor, amenities, and furnishings to match current trends and guest preferences.

Staying Competitive in Changing Markets

Airbnb isn't static, and neither should you be. Adapt to changing markets, stay aware of new competitors, and adjust your strategy accordingly.

Adapting to Travel Trends and Preferences

Travel trends change like fashion trends. Stay ahead of the curve by catering to evolving guest preferences, whether it's eco-friendly practices or work-from-anywhere setups.

Staying Informed About Airbnb Industry Trends

Finally, never stop learning. Stay informed about Airbnb industry trends through blogs, forums, and networking with fellow hosts. Knowledge is your crystal ball into the future of hosting.

Riding the Airbnb trends and seasonal peaks is like navigating a thrilling amusement park. Embrace the ups and downs, prepare for the twists and turns, and remember that, as a host, you're the conductor of your own hosting symphony. So, grab your baton and let's make some hosting magic happen!

Chapter 18:

Diversifying Your Income Streams within Airbnb

So, you've conquered the art of hosting on Airbnb and you're swimming in five-star reviews. What's next? How about turning your hosting gig into a multifaceted income extravaganza? In this chapter, we're going to explore how to diversify your income streams within the Airbnb universe.

Exploring Additional Airbnb Income Streams

Sure, bookings are great, but why stop there? Airbnb offers a multitude of income streams waiting to be tapped. Let's dive in!

Offering Experiences and Activities

Expand your horizons by offering unique experiences and activities to guests. Whether it's a cooking class, a guided hike, or a photography tour, your local expertise can translate into extra income.

Becoming an Airbnb Tour Guide

Know your city like the back of your hand? Become an Airbnb tour guide and lead guests on unforgettable adventures. Your insider knowledge is pure gold!

Selling Airbnb-Related Merchandise

Put your creativity to good use by designing and selling Airbnb-themed merchandise. Think custom mugs, T-shirts, or travel accessories. It's like hosting a souvenir shop in your own home.

Collaborating with Local Businesses

Forge partnerships with local businesses. Recommend them to your guests, and in return, negotiate commission-based deals or discounts for referrals. Win-win!

Monetizing Your Knowledge and Expertise

Are you a whiz at something specific? Offer your expertise as a paid service. Whether it's yoga classes, photography lessons, or language tutoring, your skills can become a valuable income source.

Hosting Workshops and Classes

Set up shop in your Airbnb and host workshops or classes. From painting sessions to cooking workshops, there's a world of learning that guests will pay for.

Expanding into Long-Term Rentals

While you've been excelling at short-term hosting, consider the long game. Transform your property into a long-term rental when it makes sense. It's a different income stream with its own perks.

Offering Corporate Housing Solutions

Tap into the corporate world by offering fully furnished corporate housing. Business travelers will appreciate the comfort and convenience, and you'll appreciate the steady income.

Becoming an Airbnb Consultant or Coach

Your hosting journey has made you a pro. Share your wisdom by becoming an Airbnb consultant or coach. Help new hosts kickstart their ventures, and get paid for your expertise.

Developing Affiliate Marketing Partnerships

Affiliate marketing can be a goldmine. Partner with relevant brands and promote their products or services to your guests. Earn commissions on every sale.

Exploring International Hosting Opportunities

Expand your hosting empire beyond your local borders. Consider international hosting opportunities. Collaborate with hosts in other countries to cross-promote each other's listings.

The Importance of Guest Loyalty and Repeat Bookings

Repeat guests are the Holy Grail of hosting. Provide exceptional service, build relationships, and encourage loyalty. They'll become your best marketing tool.

Evaluating the Profitability of Income Streams

Not all income streams are created equal. Evaluate the profitability of each one, considering time, effort, and expenses involved. Focus on what pays off the most.

Balancing Multiple Income Streams for Success

Diversifying your income streams is like spinning plates – you need balance. Don't spread yourself too thin; prioritize what works best for you.

Your Airbnb venture is a multifaceted gem waiting to shine. By diversifying your income streams, you not only boost your earnings but also open doors to exciting new experiences and opportunities. So, go ahead, host, teach, guide, consult, and make your Airbnb empire a symphony of income!

Chapter 19:

Marketing Your Airbnb Brand: From Local to Global

Welcome to the grand finale of your Airbnb journey – marketing your brand. It's time to shine a spotlight on your listing, draw in guests from near and far, and turn your hosting hobby into a full-fledged business. Let's dive into the magical world of Airbnb marketing!

The Role of Branding in Airbnb Success

First things first, branding isn't just for corporations. Your Airbnb venture needs its own identity, a unique flavor that sets you apart from the crowd. Why? Because branding is the gateway to guest trust and loyalty.

Defining Your Unique Selling Proposition (USP)

Why should guests choose your property over the sea of other options? Define your Unique Selling Proposition. Maybe it's your unbeatable location, your exceptional service, or your pet-friendly policy. Find your secret sauce.

Building a Memorable Airbnb Brand

Your Airbnb brand should be memorable. Pick a name, logo, and color scheme that sticks in guests' minds like a catchy tune. Think of it as crafting your hosting superhero costume.

Creating an Engaging Airbnb Profile

Your Airbnb profile is your online storefront. Fill it with captivating descriptions, high-quality photos, and eye-catching headlines. Think of it as your hosting dating profile – make guests swipe right!

Leveraging Guest Reviews and Testimonials

Good reviews are your golden ticket. Encourage guests to leave honest reviews, and showcase them like badges of honor on your listing. They're your social proof.

Utilizing Social Media for Promotion

Social media is your marketing playground. Create profiles for your Airbnb brand, post stunning photos, and engage with followers. It's like throwing a virtual housewarming party!

The Power of Content Marketing

Start a blog or YouTube channel related to your hosting area. Share local tips, travel guides, and insider knowledge. It positions you as an expert and draws in potential guests.

Building an Email List of Potential Guests

Collect email addresses from potential guests who inquire but don't book. Create a newsletter with travel tips, special offers, and local insights to keep them engaged.

Networking with Other Hosts and Businesses

Hosts unite! Network with other hosts in your area. They can refer guests to you when they're fully booked, and you can return the favor.

Collaborating with Local Influencers

Local influencers have the magic touch when it comes to drawing attention. Partner with them to showcase your property to a wider audience.

Utilizing Airbnb's Built-In Promotion Tools

Airbnb offers built-in promotion tools like discounts and special offers. Use them strategically to attract more bookings during slow periods.

Running Paid Advertising Campaigns

Invest in paid advertising, such as Google Ads or social media ads, to expand your reach. It's like putting your listing on the highway billboard of the internet.

SEO Strategies for Airbnb Listings

Learn the art of Airbnb SEO. Optimize your listing with relevant keywords and phrases to improve your ranking in search results. It's your ticket to discoverability.

Targeting Global Audiences

Don't limit yourself to local guests. Airbnb has a global audience. Consider translating your listing into multiple languages and tailoring it to different cultures.

Measuring and Analyzing Marketing Success

Don't fly blind; measure your marketing efforts' success. Use analytics tools to track website traffic, conversion rates, and booking trends. It's your marketing compass.

Marketing your Airbnb brand isn't just about shouting from the digital rooftops. It's about creating an irresistible identity, engaging with guests, and constantly fine-tuning your approach. Your brand is the heart of your hosting venture, so let it shine. Think of it as your hosting masterpiece, ready to be unveiled to the world. So, go forth, market your Airbnb brand like a pro, and watch the bookings roll in from every corner of the globe!

Conclusion

Congratulations, Airbnb Millionaire! You've embarked on a remarkable journey, and it's time to reflect on the incredible adventure you've just experienced.

Reflecting on Your Airbnb Journey

Think back to when you first opened your doors to guests, the excitement, the anticipation, and maybe a hint of nervousness. You've come a long way since then, transforming your space into a thriving source of income and adventure.

The Transformation into an Airbnb Millionaire

Yes, you read that right! You are now part of an exclusive club – the Airbnb Millionaires. Your property, your savvy hosting skills, and your dedication have brought you wealth beyond your initial dreams.

Celebrating Your Achievements

Take a moment to celebrate your achievements. You've mastered the art of hosting, expanded your income streams, and built a memorable brand. These are no small feats.

The Lifelong Learning and Growth Continuum

Remember, the journey doesn't end here. Hosting is a lifelong learning experience. Continue to seek knowledge, adapt to changing trends, and refine your hosting skills.

Your Role in the Airbnb Community

As an Airbnb Millionaire, you're not just a successful host; you're a part of a global community. Share your knowledge, mentor others, and contribute to the growth of this incredible platform.

The End is Just the Beginning

This isn't a conclusion; it's a new beginning. Your path to success is a never-ending adventure. There are more guests to host, more experiences to create, and more wealth to accumulate.

Final Thoughts and Encouragement

Don't let challenges deter you; let them inspire you. Remember that every hurdle is an opportunity to learn and grow. Embrace the ups and downs of hosting, for they are all part of the journey.

The Future of Airbnb Wealth

The future of Airbnb wealth is bright. As the sharing economy continues to evolve, new opportunities will arise. Stay adaptable, stay innovative, and keep an eye on the horizon.

Your Continued Path to Success

Your success story is far from over. Continue to set goals, refine your strategies, and, most importantly, take action. Success is not a destination; it's a journey.

Thanking Your Readers and Supporters

A big thank you to all the readers and supporters who have joined you on this Airbnb Millionaire journey. Your success is made even sweeter when shared with others.

Taking Action on Your Airbnb Dreams

You've read this book, absorbed its wisdom, and now it's time to take action. Turn your dreams into reality. Whether you're starting fresh or refining your existing hosting venture, remember that every small step counts.

Stay Inspired and Keep Hosting

Hosting on Airbnb is not just about money; it's about experiences, connections, and personal growth. Stay inspired by the stories of your guests, and keep welcoming the world into your space.

Never Stop Innovating and Improving

The world of Airbnb is dynamic, and so should be your hosting approach. Innovate, adapt, and continuously improve. Your commitment to excellence will keep your guests coming back.

Gratitude for the Airbnb Millionaire Experience

As you reflect on your journey, remember to cultivate gratitude. Gratitude for the opportunities Airbnb has brought your way, for the lessons learned, and for the financial freedom achieved.

The Journey Continues: Your Financial Destiny Awaits!

In the world of Airbnb, the journey never truly ends. Your financial destiny is yours to shape. Keep dreaming, keep hosting, and keep building the life you desire. Your path to wealth and success awaits, Airbnb Millionaire. Go forth and conquer it!

www.ingramcontent.com/pod-product-compliance
Lightning Source LLC
Chambersburg PA
CBHW062325290526
45794CB00005B/1896